# CONTACT: THEORY ★ LUSTRUM PRESS

770.92
C.759

ALL RIGHTS RESERVED UNDER INTERNATIONAL AND PAN-AMERICAN COPYRIGHT CONVENTIONS.
PUBLISHED IN THE UNITED STATES OF AMERICA BY LUSTRUM PRESS, INC.,
BOX 450, CANAL STREET STATION, NEW YORK, NEW YORK 10013
COPYRIGHT © 1980 BY LUSTRUM PRESS, INC.
JOHN FLATTAU, RALPH GIBSON AND ARNE LEWIS

———————

DISTRIBUTED IN GREAT BRITAIN BY TRAVELLING LIGHT PHOTOGRAPHY LIMITED
MANUFACTURED IN THE UNITED STATES OF AMERICA
LIBRARY OF CONGRESS CATALOGUE CARD NUMBER: 80-7809
ISBN: 0-912810-30-0 (HARDCOVER): 0-912810-31-9 (PAPER)

———————

TYPOGRAPHY BY THE STUART FINE CORPORATION
PRINTED BY RAPOPORT PRINTING CORPORATION
BOUND BY SENDOR BINDERY
DESIGNED BY ARNE LEWIS

———————

ELEVEN IS SILVER

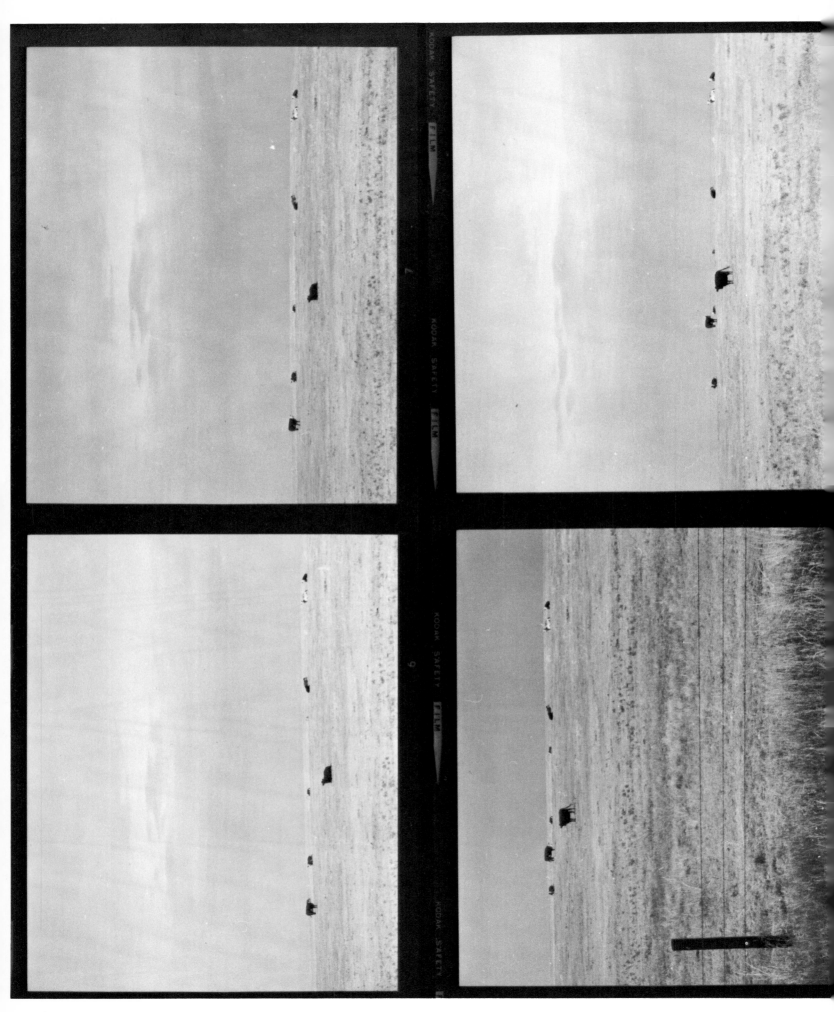

4

ROBERT ADAMS

With roll film I spend as much time studying the contacts as I do taking the pictures. I wish I were able, of course, to get things right when I make the exposures, but when I use small cameras it's because the subject is elusive and has to be shot first and thought about later. Anyway, studying a contact is pretty much like studying the ground glass—both are attempts to see as completely as you can.

I work on contacts with cardboard L's (the L's are cut from file folders, which are pliable and opaque). The first thing I want to learn about a picture is its structure, whether it's going to stand up, and for that one has to see it by itself.

I don't crop often or much.

The idea of a pair of cow pictures occurred to me only after I saw the contact, maybe because the pictures were made over a span of fifteen minutes or so (negotiations with range cattle are delicate).

At home when I saw the two frames, that's when the work started. The light had changed between the exposures, but to emphasize the shifting of the cows I wanted everything else to seem nearly the same, so the tones had to be balanced in the final prints.

As for the cows themselves, setting aside this technical talk, they make me smile. Though all that space around them is perhaps a little sobering. I remember a funny story a friend told me from her childhood on the prairie near Sterling, Colorado: she'd gone to the outhouse but didn't come back, and when her parents went to check they discovered that a cow had laid down against the door! The comic improbability is wonderful. Though it also reminds one of the central fact of plains life—a vast and empty landscape that makes nearly everything improbable. But cows don't read Kierkegaard; we love them for their certitude.

ROBERT ADAMS

8

JEAN-PHILIPPE CHARBONNIER

In October, 1944, in the small town of Vienne (Isere), France, a French collaborator named Nitard was sentenced to death.

He was no large-scale spy—just a man who had been working as a clerk in the German administration, probably for the Gestapo. But one must remember that in the early days of Liberation in France, as in any other country that had suffered four years' occupation, feelings ran high against any collaborator, big or small. And then, of course, the really dangerous collaborators were not easy to bring to justice so the small fry had to pay the price for their more fortunate partners-in-crime. More fuel to the fire had been the executions by the Germans of many great patriots both in Lyons and in Vienne.

The outcry was therefore so violent that, even though Nitard's appeal to the Courts of Justice in Grenoble had been successful, the shooting was ordered to take place, so as not to disappoint the population of Vienne, I cannot help feeling.

So that everyone in the town should have a chance to watch the execution and share in the general revenge, it was scheduled to take place at noon. Five thousand people, children included, crowded into the square in front of the old military barracks. So intense was the excitement that one could almost smell it as one can before a bullfight or even a good football game, while in the barrack square the condemned man gulped back the traditional glass of rum and lit the traditional cigarette. He puffed at it a few times, then stubbed it out, thrust the butt into his pocket and went to face the firing-squad.

He passed through a hall where the twelve rifles, one with a blank cartridge, had been laid out ready, and walked out into the square to be met by a priest, the firing-squad, its commanding officer and the now strangely silent crowd.

This demonstration of public justice shocked me profoundly. No one deplored collaboration more than I but this punishment seemed to me to be out of all proportion to this man's relatively small crime. My nerves were taut. This man who was about to die was so close. I don't remember whether the crowd was silent now or not. I only know that I set my Leica automatically, as in a dream…or rather, a nightmare. Subconscious reflexes turned my battered old Summar F2 lens to the closest possible range while I tried to fight off feelings of disgust.

Suddenly I felt very close to that man standing alone in the square. The cigarette butt. Injustice to humanity. And then the overwhelming feeling that the man was dead already, that he was like a duck with its head cut off that runs for minutes before finally falling dead. He was dead before he ever entered that "arena"—even after fifteen years I can't stand using that word.

The "show" was reaching its climax but now the man was untied from the post. He was a traitor and traitors are not given the right to meet death facing the squad. The seconds ticked by as he was bound with his back to the rifles. And then they fired.

Nitard never saw me although I was at times no more than five feet away. The whole story took up just one 35mm roll, as you can see—the biggest, most compact story I ever covered and one I wish never to have to cover again.

JEAN-PHILIPPE CHARBONNIER

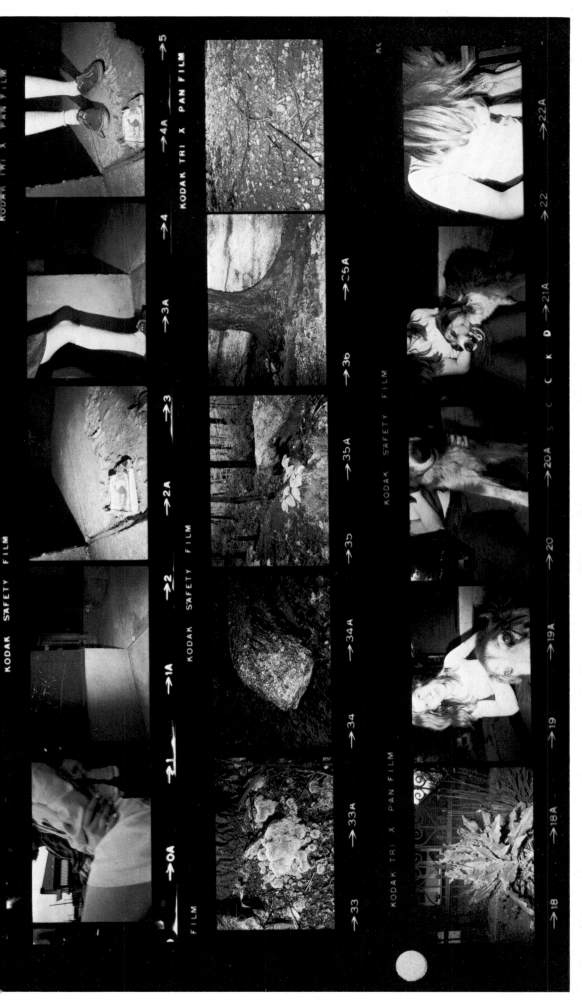

MARK COHEN

I'm not too interested in contact sheets, except as a record keeping system. This sheet is made up of three or four rolls. Before I develop the film I have distinct ideas about which pictures I will want to print. When the film is dry I like to make the prints as soon as possible. I can tell from the negative how the print will look by looking at it on a light table and using a magnifying glass. The sequence that begins with frame No. 1 and ends with frame No. 4 shows that I took two pictures with a flash while I waited for the girl with white knee socks to get closer to the background I selected. When she was close enough I took frame No. 3. Then she stopped and I took one more of her sneaks, that seemed to assure her that she was not threatened.

MARK COHEN

WILLIAM COUPON

The reason for my picking this particular negative was that it most conveyed that which I was most concerned with in regards to this subject—a simple elegance.

I usually insist on an element of arrogance, sometimes very understated. This way, I can give weak faces strength. The right combination of vulnerability and strength has to be within the chosen negative, especially within a portrait situation. Here, the combination involved an aloof androgyny. That way it retained its elegance quietly.

Also, the design of this photograph was instrumental—a centered detachment of "frilless" elegance.

WILLIAM COUPON

20

JUDY DATER

Twinka 1970

At least thirty 4x5 negatives were made on this particular day sometime in 1970. We worked in several locations. This contact sheet shows only four photographs taken in this one setting in front of a redwood tree in my back yard. There were 12 shots in all. The picture that I chose to print, the one in the upper left corner, was the only possible choice.

My initial reaction to this photograph was that it was too hard, too theatrical, perhaps overly dramatic, and it scared me a little. It took me a few weeks to finally make a print. I kept coming back to it and my attraction to this image soon won out over any misgivings I might have had at first. None of the other pictures had the same power. The haunting expression in the eyes, the skeletal outline of the skull showing through the flesh of the face, combined with the striking features were irresistible. Most of all her intense confrontation with the camera/viewer/ photographer was important and essential.

The dress, which belonged to a friend of the model, with its sheer gauzelike material, puffy sleeves, ribbon and velvet rose is explicitly feminine. It serves as a counterpoint to the tension in her arm and hands. The dress simultaneously accentuates and conceals her body.

This portrait goes beyond and underneath the surface beauty of the model. Twinka is unquestionably a very attractive woman, and infinitely complex as a person. This picture of her reflects some of that intricate essence of character that first attracted me to Twinka, and made me want to photograph her. She is much more than beautiful. Only a portrait that shows some of what is inside as well as what's outside would satisfy me.

JUDY DATER

BEVAN DAVIES

25

Contact prints are the proof that I did something wrong. Perhaps I could have moved the camera two feet this way or that, or waited until the sun was in a slightly different position. They show how difficult the medium can be.

In a more positive way, they are a guide to the seasons, to the way light hits certain buildings at different times of the year. Contacts have made me change my procedures somewhat, insofar as I now do as many as four different views of a subject, ending up with more than one successful photograph many times. By looking at my contact prints I can often retrace my steps around a subject—the nice thing about buildings is they stay put—and this will enable me to go back to the essential thing I missed, and if I'm lucky, make a better picture.

I always feel apprehensive about making contact prints because they finalize your ideas and take some of the magic away from the picture-making process.

These two photographs were made on the same day, within a few feet of each other, and yet are very different. The vertical one seemed less like things I had done before, and interesting enough to make a large print. I always make 16x20 prints because it widens the range of middle tones, and I prefer to see detail in every area of a photograph. The contacts are harsh and block up shadow detail and white areas. Somehow the scale of the subjects is not very effective in a small print, and often small details in the photographs are important, but barely visible in the contact.

So, the contact print for me is the unhappy moment of truth, but the door that can open onto possibilities.

BEVAN DAVIES

27

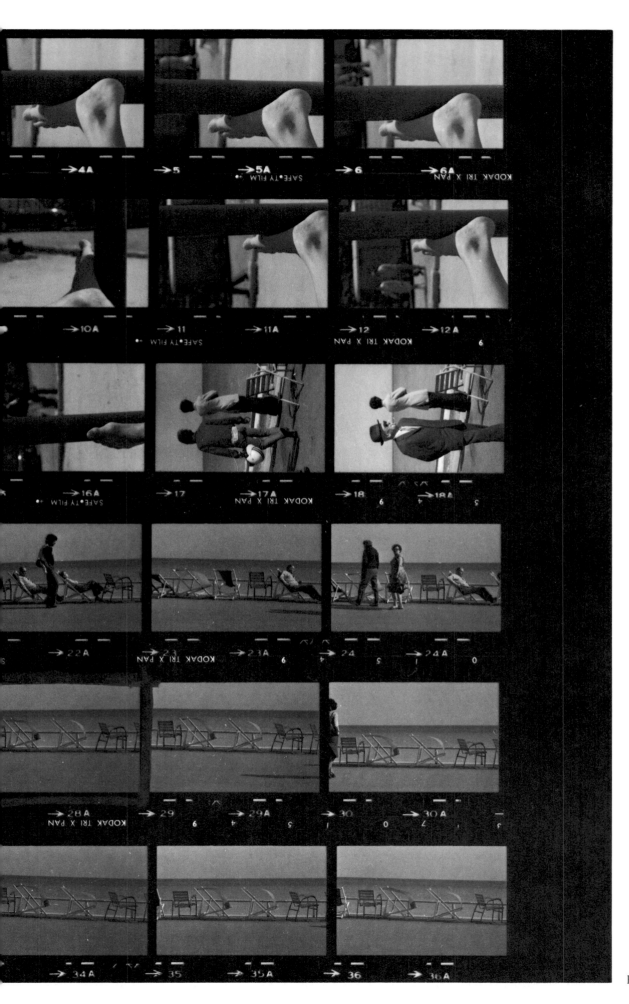

ELLIOT ERWITT

Contact sheets should be as private as a toothbrush and ought to be guarded as jealously as a mistress. They should never be published; they should be seen only by one's closest, benevolent associate when the photographer is stuck in a decision about which specific picture to use and cannot resolve it himself.

A dozen contact sheets tell far more about a photographer than a dozen "good" pictures taken by that same photographer. Two dozen contact sheets taken at random from various stories and carefully scrutinized would be equal to a complete (photographic) psychoanalysis of the photographer.

Contact sheets reveal how one thinks and how one sees. They remove the mystery of how one gets to a finished picture. They are bad for our carefully cultivated mystique.

How cunning of the editor of this book to get so many of us to take down our drawers in public! Shame on him.

ELLIOTT ERWITT

NATHAN FARB

It seems to me that before I tell you how I use my contact sheets, it would be useful for you to have an understanding of how I view photography and that would establish a context in which either to accept or discard my ideas.

Simply put, I have always felt that photography, or at least what I think of as the important photography in this century, is more related to literature than it is to painting. On the most simple and intimate level, the contact sheets are my diaries, and my notebooks. In some crude way, they represent a raw unedited truth, not as finely shaped or as elegantly stated as the final product, but more basic and perhaps more honest in the long run, than those finished products that have so much time and effort poured into them to create and protect my own image and one might even say ego, in the analytic sense of that term.

On a second and perhaps even simpler level one can view the contact sheets as the whole work and the edited, or shown, or published part of the work only the tip of the iceberg.

I sometimes take this very mechanistic view and would actually like to see my contact sheets published. Other times, I think I would be quite embarrassed were this to happen. However, currently in working with the Russian contact sheets, I marvel at all the wonderful pictures that did not get published. It's hard to know whether this is simply narcissistic self involvement or a statement of real validity. Having questioned it, let us pursue it for a moment. Let us say that the almost 400 contact sheets with some 1500 people are considerably more interesting than the 80 pictures that were finally distilled into a book from that body of work. No doubt, there are a few of you who would like to see the entire set; who would be willing to sit and study them with the same time, effort and enjoyment that it takes to read a good novel. Undoubtedly we are arriving at a stage in the history of this medium where serious and scholarly people are acknowledging its value, but on the whole that is still far too few people to publish a book for, so we are back to the real problem of how to use those contact sheets, distill them and produce a coherent work of art that can be grasped on a fast 10 minute lookthrough and yet have substance for a week-long study.

The editing—the pondering over—is the long and tedious job and therefore each contact sheet must be made well. If they are printed poorly the study of them, twice or three times as tedious, wears one out before completion of the task. Every frame must be printed well. There is no room for frames that are too light. It's like having notebooks or diaries in which one can only read every 5th word. In general I agree with almost all other photographers who say make them dark, and if you have to, put them on a lightbox to see what they would look like printed lighter.

I find that taking my contact sheets to bed with me (much as I do with a book or magazine) is good. I have time to think about them, to daydream, to live with them so to speak. It does not replace the work of sitting at a desk and marking them and taking notes, but it is invaluable to come to an understanding of what is on the sheets and what can be done with them.

Then there are the stages of making the rough cut and then the final smooth edit, terms which are much more frequently used in film. Simply put, that means taking 200 pictures out of 2000 and trying to make them say what the 2000 did and then bringing it down to a final eighty or ninety. Every body of work flows from a different place inside and requires different tactics and methodology. I can briefly recite what I did with the Russian photographs because it is fresh in my mind. I was trying to show a cross section of people of the Soviet Union—not an exact sociological one, but one that you or I might encounter walking around a large city. Since I was dealing with social types, I would try to see what a certain picture represented that no other picture did, and second, determine how many other pictures that one picture represented. For example, if I felt that one picture said what it took two or three others to say, that became an important choice.

The contact sheets came under closer and closer scrutiny. I got stuck. I called up a friend or two to help me. Tom Ridinger, an editor at CAMERA ART, who has looked at hundreds of thousands of pictures and still loves to look at more helped me over the most difficult part. We sat for about two weeks analyzing each sheet and out of that I was able to make some clear decisions. I am not suggesting that one casually show your contact sheets around, or that you lean on anyone else to do your editing and shaping. That is a cop out, but going to someone you trust with your sheets is productive and is an integral, and finally, important part of the process.

NATHAN FARB

LOUIS FAURER

I worked on these photographs between 1937 and 1947. The photographs were originally exposed with either a Leica or a Rolleiflex. When I work with the 35mm, the image is usually best full-frame, but whenever necessary I will crop. When it's all there, the image fills the frame. I am interested in and have been influenced by all of twentieth century art.

The image reproduced was photographed on the Staten Island Ferry.

Looking at a contact sheet, when I see something good, I feel as though it is almost a miracle. I make full negative roughs. I stamp them "rough print". Sometimes a contact print doesn't look so good but the rough print surprises me. On rare occasions the opposite is true.

LOUIS FAURER

MARK FELDSTEIN

The memory of the image seen through the camera remains with me for a long time after the exposure. The interval between my taking and my developing/proofing an image ranges from hours to weeks. I carry these visual memories internally and upon developing/proofing I am confronted with the actuality of the film recorded image. The time interval between the exposure and the first concretization of the image is for me a magical time and a kind of gestation period. Some remembered moments I know will continue as prints, others I'm less certain of and need more time to consider; while still others are rejected even as memories. The negative/proof coexists with my internal image of the moment photographed. In some instances there is a clear correspondence between the two while in others what the proof reveals is less compelling than my memory. Some images which puzzle me as memories seem to resolve themselves during the gestation and are realized by the contact sheet. The proof is for me a personal route map, an indication of my travels, state of mind and relationship to my subject. I can follow bits of my visual past, present and perhaps future. The proof causes me to chronologically re-live that morning or day when I made the exposure.

I project those among the proofed negatives that I want to pursue. A small number of the total of projected images are printed. I printly slowly and work with the relationships between the memory and the proof sheet and the new possibilities generated by their dialogue.

I walk and bicycle in Manhattan a great deal, returning to old haunts and exploring new locations. The diner in frames 1-4 had eluded me visually for years. I can trace my own changes in images made from it over the last several years. There is slight exposure bracketing between frames 1-4 as well as variations in both focus and aperture. I chose frame 5 as the placement of point of focus provided the greatest depth of field. I used a wide angle lens to form the space and to cover a great field of view. The mid-morning sun makes all the silvery surfaces glisten and dematerialize in spite of their mass and volume. The silvery quality of the surfaces and the undulation of the spatial planes intrigues me as it creates a sense of paradox. The image is both heavy and light, flat and deep. The sky is both void and solid and the building at infinity is both in the distance and in the same plane as the foreground. These paradoxes interact visually and make the situation unreal and fantastic. The other frames of the diner are far more literal and involve a less ambiguous space. Their volumes retain their mass and function as barriers for the viewer. There is no seductive aspect to the landscape. The remainder of the frames on the roll are all aspects of the same building. The images are far less complex spatially; they have deep spatial thrusts and dramatic perspective but are not as evocative of the interaction between picture-plane, light, space, mass and surface as the frame that I chose to print. The frame I printed transcends the physical subject.

MARK FELDSTEIN

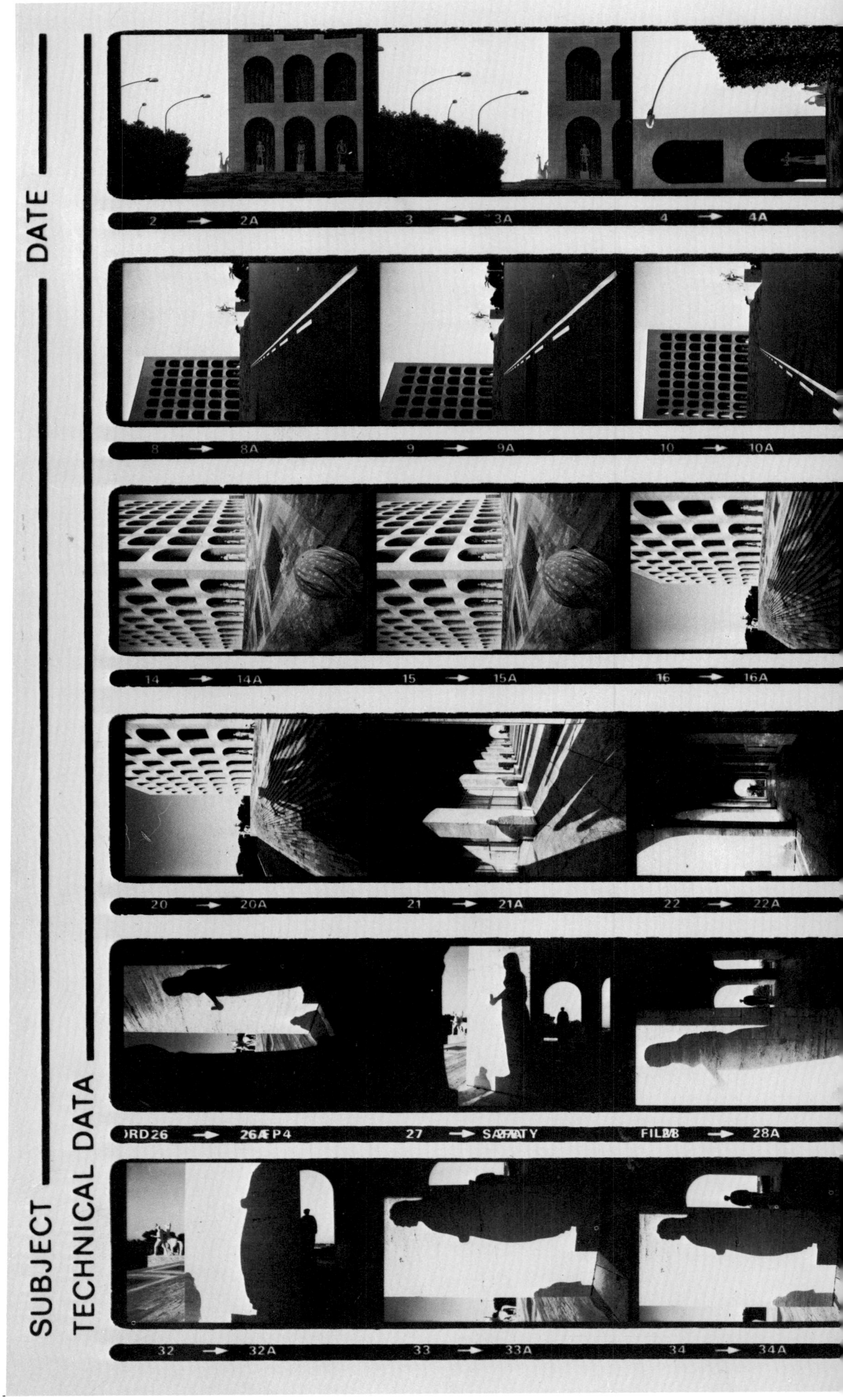
SUBJECT
TECHNICAL DATA
DATE
2 → 2A 3 → 3A 4 → 4A
8 → 8A 9 → 9A 10 → 10A
14 → 14A 15 → 15A 16 → 16A
20 → 20A 21 → 21A 22 → 22A
32 → 32A 33 → 33A 34 → 34A

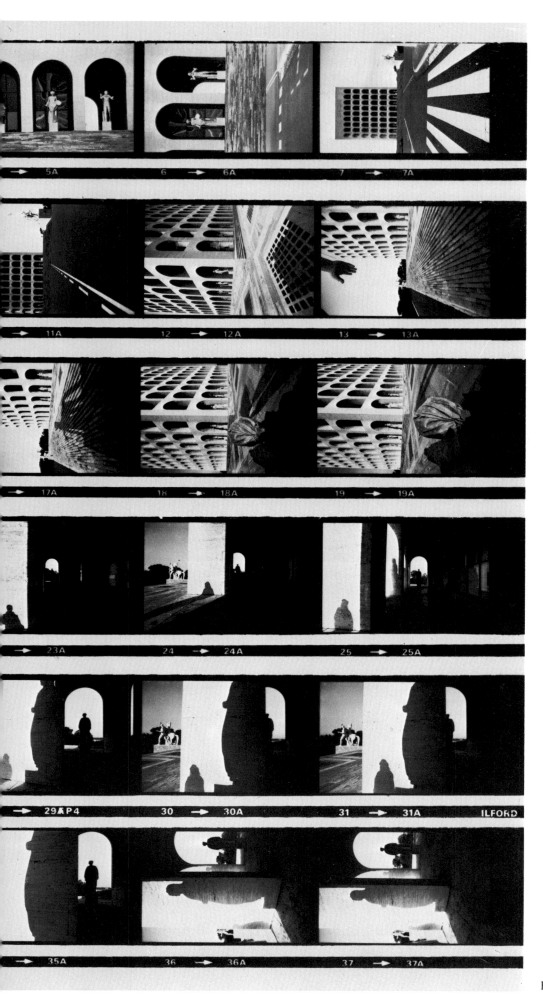

FRANCO FONTANA

I think that to photograph is to violate reality, because reality does not exist in an absolute sense, or it exists only in a metaphysical sense, as a universal principle, which however is evaded in our daily experience: this experience dominated by the habit of rational analysis, kills our imagination preventing it from giving to things significances which are not the habitual ones.

The imagination is the great force which provokes, stimulates and sets in motion the images, giving life to them, penetrating the opaque surfaces of things. The objects and the situations we photograph are only a pretense to speak about our inner experiences and it is our story which is shown through them: a lamp is not just a lamp but it becomes a part of us the moment we see it.

That which renders an image fascinating is the violence from which it is born. That violence which is necessary to get rid of all the habits clipping our gaze. It is necessary to exercise a violence so as not to allow things to use ourselves, because it is we who are the bearers of the only meaning to which we can be witness, while the presumed "objective" meaning is destined ever to escape us.

The work I have done for this occasion seems to me to be representative enough of this way of thinking, even if there is some disparity between our intentions and the results. There is always the camera in the middle with all its limitations that prevents the full invention which alone could permit a true dialogue with our neighbour.

As it can be seen from the first test contact images, initially I let myself be influenced by the place I had chosen: they are timid images which remain at the surface; but then I took heart again and with caution I began to try to go beyond the surface of things. I feel that the operation here described is a work of abstraction: abstraction is for me "overcoming the automatic consciousness, the common consciousness."

It is this operation which gives me emotion, but it is an emotion accompanied by the anxiety of trying to succeed in capturing it in the picture. Only when I am in front of the test images this anxiety can be placated. Thus, having become a spectator of myself, I can proceed with absolute calm to relive the emotions which I experienced in such a tumultuous way, and to select the photogram which seems to me to restore those emotions in the best way.

FRANCO FONTANA

G.F. 3913 — Le Brusc. Piscine conçue par Alain
Capeillères.
"Vacances des Français" Pour Fondation de la Photo.

48

MARTINE FRANCK

49

I have certain misgivings about letting my contact sheet be published but in final analysis I realize that I am curious to see how other photographers work. Frankly I am a little scared that the result is disappointing. It is not that I have any secrets to hide but all of a sudden the whole procedure of photographing becomes banal and rather ponderous. I think one must never forget that it is the result that counts and not how one obtains that result. I do however make a distinction between those photographs that are "created" and those that are "found". I have been asked on several occasions whether this particular picture was "set up", all I can say is that if I had staged it, it would probably have been better but this would have been impossible because to start with I would never have had the imagination to create such an image.

This picture was taken during the summer of 1976. I had just been given a grant by the Fondation Nationale de la Photographie along with Guy Le Querrec, Claude Raimond Dityvon, Francois Hers and Daniel Jouhanneau to photograph the French on holiday. I was on my way to photograph a pop and rock festival at Le Castellet and decided to stop by and see my friend the architect Alain Capeilleres. I knew that Alain had just completed the swimming-pool, he had talked about its conception the previous year and I was really excited to see it. He greeted me by saying that an Italian photographer had just come to take photographs for an architectural review and that I should go down to the pool and have a swim. I saw a couple of people doing exercises and an empty hammock and then all of a sudden a young boy got into the hammock, the first thing I noticed was the shadow and I ran. It was all over so quickly I remember trying to find the best angle and being bothered by a towel on the left of the hammock and a bathing suit on the right, then Alain's wife Lucie arrived in her sun hat, said hello to the young boy. A few seconds later another boy climbed into the hammock. I changed angles but the picture was gone.

I had Tri X in my camera and I distinctly remember being concerned by the glare of the August midday sun on the white tilings. I had closed down to f.16 and was shooting at a 1000th of a second but I still knew I was going to be over exposed, however most important I was convinced I had an image.

The ultimate choice was easy. Frame 18a was discarded because of the towel on the left, the figures in the background were confused and I had framed too close to the shadow of the hammock. Frame 16a was a possibility but I would have had to crop the bathing suit on the right which I preferred not to do and the man doing push ups in the background was in a less interesting position. The image that had the greatest intensity and concision was to my mind frame 17a.

One rarely expresses in words all the random thoughts that run through one's head except maybe on a psychoanalyst's couch and yet the contact sheet spares neither the viewer nor the photographer. I feel that by allowing myself to be violated and by publishing that which is most intimate I am taking the very real risk of breaking the spell of destroying a certain mystery.

I would like to add in conclusion that the world around us does have rare moments of unimaginable beauty and emotion that one can sometimes capture if one is lucky, on the look out and in this case prepared to run.

MARTINE FRANCK

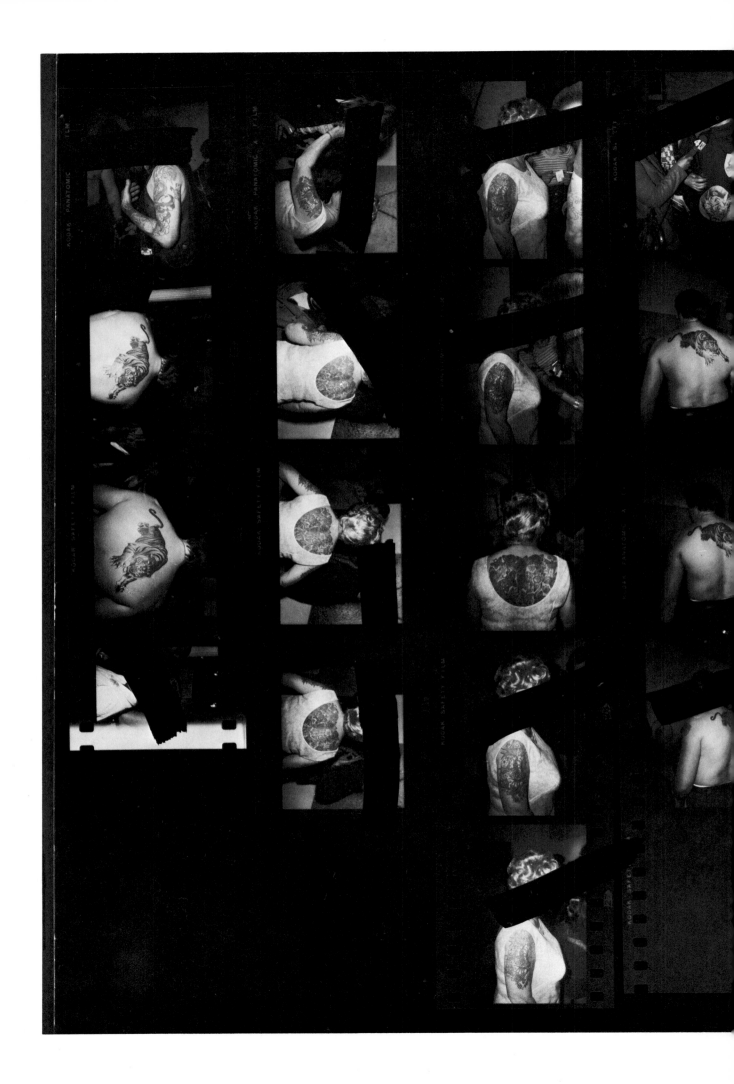

CHARLES GATEWOOD

53

This is the first roll of a take from an opening in April, 1976, at the Levitan Gallery in Soho, featuring new work by tattoo artist Spider Webb. This was my first meeting with Spider, and our mutual rapport was instantaneous. Curiously, this photograph, and the others I took this day, led to the publication of a book some 3½ years later.

I know this is the first roll because the first frame shows my cat sitting on the dishwasher at my loft. The second frame, taken at the gallery, shows a heavily tattooed back done by Spider. The 7th through the 10th frames show a frontal view of the same subject.

By frame 11 I have met Lord Balkin, an extraordinarily striking figure in a long black cape, wearing one of Spider's most unusual and important works, a rare facial tattoo with special occult meanings, an inverted pentagram. Spider later told me that Balkin had seen the symbol in a vision, and asked that it be permanently placed on his forehead.

I asked Balkin to pose for a picture, and took frames 11-13. I then spotted a huge photographic blowup of a man's nipple with a circle tattooed around it, and posed Balkin in front for an additional 4 frames, asking him to stoop slightly to frame his head in the circle, thus adding a tattooed halo to his already otherwordly appearance.

The other shots on the roll are not uninteresting, particularly frames 10 and 26. Yet this particular image is my favorite from that day, and indeed from the thousands of subsequent tattoo taken for what eventually grew into the collaborative book: SPIDER WEBB'S PUSHING INK: THE FINE ART OF TATTOOING, published in 1979. That this image should stand out so strongly is in many ways amazing, since I spent less than 60 seconds with Balkin, and have not encountered him since.

The techniques here are simple and straightforward: straight flash, Panatomic-X film, rated at 64 ASA and developed in D-76, 1:1. The negative was rich, clean, and snappy. In printing, I cropped the frame slightly and evened the background. The final print, on Polycontrast F Rapid, shows a rich tonal range, perfect contrast, and exquisite detail; a timeless portrait of a modern-day Rasputin.

CHARLES GATEWOOD

RALPH GIBSON

This image was made in Venice, Jan. 1980. The pillar is in front of the Teatro Fenice, the old opera palace, and the atmosphere was redolent of Comedia del Arte. After shooting we went inside for a performance of "THE TURK IN ITALY." Using the new Polaroid 600 SE system was a new experience for me and I welcomed the opportunity to see the images progress in the positive/negative stages. Type 665 film is medium speed, ASA 75, and the low light called for a tripod. This enabled me to refine the camera angle and exposure through gradual steps leading to the final result. The peel off print would be fine but the negative slightly thin, so I gave an additional stop exposure to yield a rich negative for printing on conventional paper. Contact prints are generally my weakest link in the creative process. I often feel that there is some important image being overlooked and I print contacts on the contrasty side to give them a closer resemblance to the final print. I believe that contact prints track my line of thought.

Looking over old sheets I can recall subtleties and variations of incidents that would otherwise be forgotten. They are a kind of memory bank and for that reason I keep them carefully filed.

RALPH GIBSON

JOHN GOSSAGE

The question of contact sheets for me is really a question of editing. I would first like to discuss why the pictures on this roll of film were made in this way.

These pictures are part of a commissioned project for the Seattle Arts Commission, to photograph for thirty days within the city limits. I'd been working for about 2 weeks on this project before these pictures were made. By this time I'd familiarized myself quite well with the city. This day I'd decided to work on the problem of making a number of views standing on the side of one hill looking off to the horizon of the next. I'd also had a fairly good idea of the exact area I'd wished to work in. The contact sheet reflects about 3-5 minutes walking time and a fairly coldblooded attitude toward the material in that I had quite a good idea of what I wished to do before I'd arrived.

The repetition of frames of the same scene is primarily done to insure a single quality negative of each scene, in that most negatives that I shoot are at quite small apertures and therefore in turn require somewhat treacherous shutter speeds. The first thing I check for after my general interest in the negative, is whether camera shake is at all a problem. The negative from which the reproduction in this book was made, was shot at either f/32 or f/45 at a 1/60 or 1/30 of a second. In this particular case all three frames are acceptably sharp. So the deciding factor in choosing this photograph is the inclusion in the upper right hand corner of a small bit of foliage that completes my intentions for the pictures arrangement.

For making decisions from my contact sheets, I'll use a piece of 8 x 10 paper with an opening cut in it's center to the size of a single frame in this case 2¼ x 2¾. It helps me to isolate each picture and make my decisions without the other frames distracting me. After a frame is chosen, I make a proof print about 8 x 10. If the image survives a week or so of viewing and still keeps my interest I will then make exhibition prints from the negative.

JOHN GOSSAGE

PAUL HILL

Although my reliance on selecting from a contact sheet is nowhere as great as it was when I was a photojournalist, I still find that 'the way' is frequently illuminated by my contacts. I always learn from my contact sheets although I think deciphering negatives is more important than reading contacts, as the negative gives you much more relevant photographic information. Even the most carefully printed contact sheet will only give you half the story.

The comparative precision I use in my image-making nowadays means that I do not shoot a great deal of film. I have noticed that I average around 2 successes per film, but then I have been photographing for 20 years so I should be getting reasonably proficient by now. I can never understand those photographers who tell you how many miles of film they have shot or how many contact sheets they have to wade through before they mention the actual pictures!

This contact sheet of some bulk-loaded film (I mention this just in case the numbers on the film confuse you) was taken in November 1976 in the area around my workshop in Derbyshire, England. It contains two of my favourite images (frames 20 & 27), but more importantly it highlights pre-visualization and post-visualization. Frame 27 was one of those delightful discoveries that come along occasionally when you are shooting. I knew as soon as my daughter turned her head to the right, thus casting a shadow like a man's head, that it would 'make it'. I could never have worked out this picture in my imagination in advance because the formation of the wall, the posture of my daughter and the angle of light that helped cast the telling shadow, were unique to that place at that particular time. Nobody had ever seen or made that image before me. It also fitted into the sort of work I was doing then, so the joy was doubled. Although I took some more shots around the same location (the wall was of a private house—I was attracted by the shadows initially), I intuitively knew that frame 27 was likely to be the best.

When I think I have found 'the elusive image', I usually shoot a few frames of the same subject matter (sometimes varying the exposures and depth of field, if time allows) so I have a choice of frames just in case one gets scratched or screwed-up somehow.

The transposition of the 3D world into two dimensions in the photographer's mind's eye is never easy. Sometimes you can easily imagine the final print and be pretty accurate (as in frame 27), but on other occasions you only realise what is going on when you examine the sheet (as with frame 20).

When your photographs can teach you something you did not know or when they give you a visual experience you have never enjoyed before, its wonderfully satisfying to be a photographer.

PAUL HILL

68

EVELYN HOFER

When I was asked by John Loengard, the picture editor of LIFE MAGAZINE, to take a portrait of Ted Kennedy, I decided that I wanted to take a very close view of his face and have his eyes look straight at me. I also wanted him to be serious and not laugh. So this was what I worked on during the actual sitting. The contact prints, therefore, all look very similar. Some seem to be identical, however as I worked on the enlargements, I realized that only one, No. 13, was really the one I thought best.

EVELYN HOFER

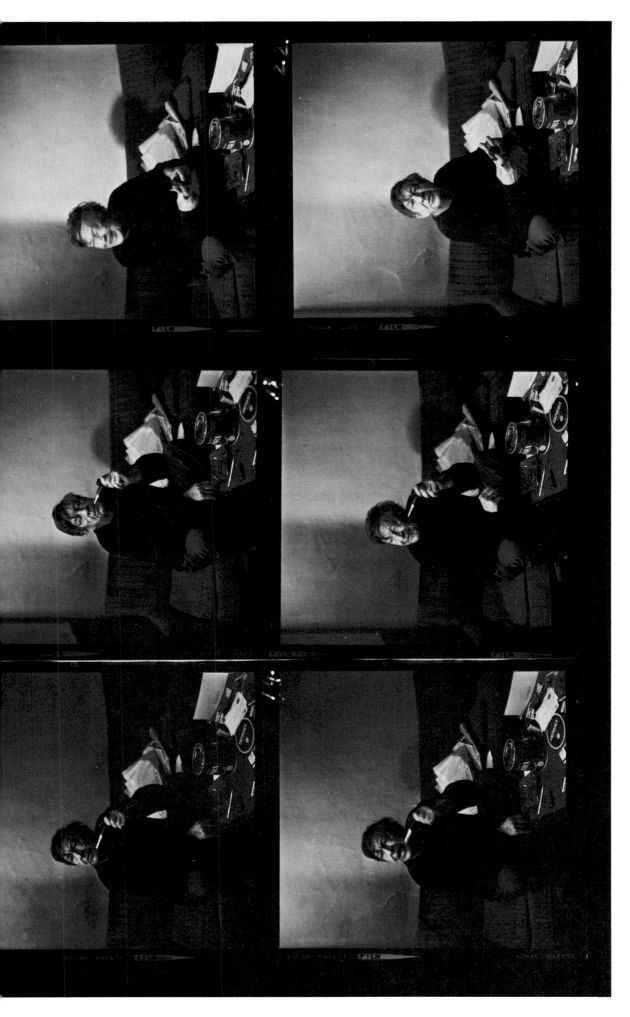

HORST

Photographing W.H. Auden was done very casually
during an afternoon's conversation at his house in
Greenwich Village. I had no preconceived idea and
shot with available light. While I normally contact
everything I shoot I'm used to having a picture editor
make the final selection. I might make a suggestion
once in a while but generally refrain. When I have to
choose I find it often difficult to pick the right one, but
this one, frame number 17, is the one I liked the best.

HORST

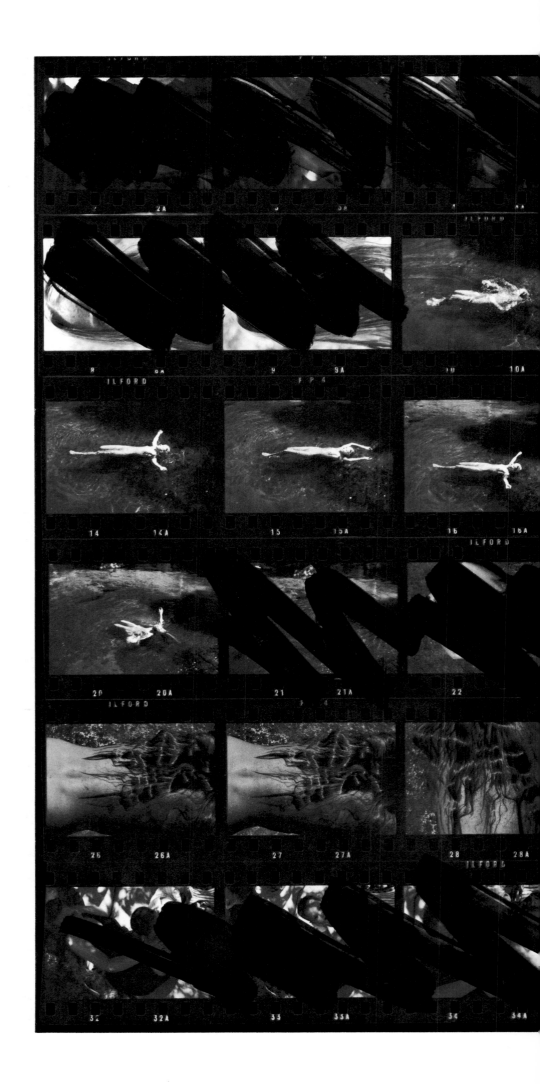

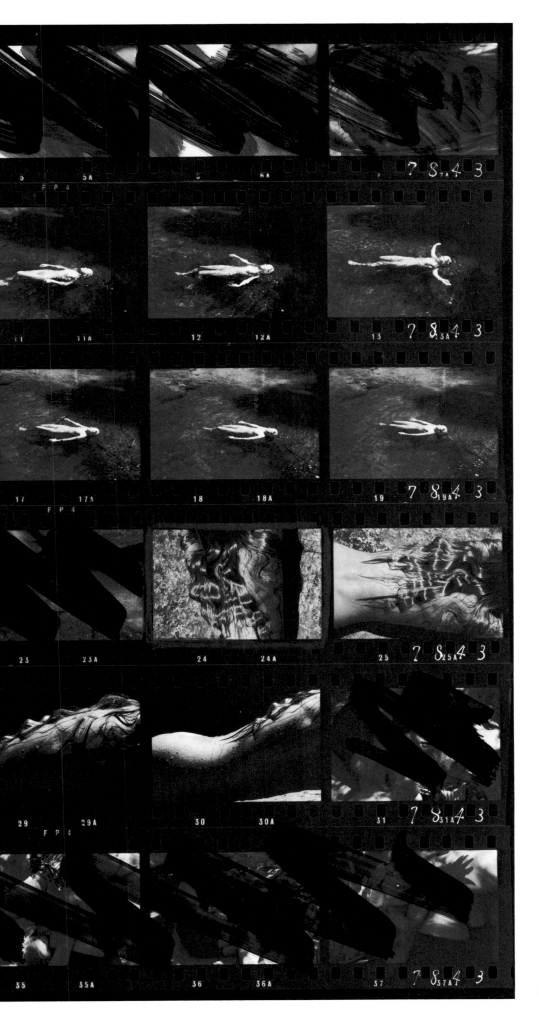

EIKOH HOSOE

About the selected print from the contact

This was taken in the summer of 1975 at Yosemite on the occasion of the Ansel Adams Workshop where I participated as one of the instructors with Wynn Bullock, Imogen Cunningham, Robert Heinecken, Lucien Clergue, Jack Welpott, Judy Dater, etc.

It was a nude workshop that many of the nude models were young photography students, male and female, who participated the workshop mainly as models but part-time photographers. Before lunch time every photography student concentrated to shoot the nude models, and the nude models had no time to change their positions to be photographers, but after lunch—it happened almost every time—the clothed students except for a few of them undressed their jeans and T-shirts and jumped into the water pool in the valley with the naked models as the sun comes to the head of us. The clothed photographers including the instructors were jealous of the naked models because it looked so natural and free to be naked in the nature like Yosemite. First I hestitated to undress though I wanted, but I finally unclothed because I had to. It was because I fell into the water pool from the top of the slippery rock about twenty feet high, running with the water fall holding a camera with me, and then I became naked but my poor camera got wet with water and never worked any more. I soon realised that a naked man should not bring his camera and walk or jump from a rock to a rock because his balancing balls cause a camera-blurr. Why? you will see if you take a serious photograph when you are naked. You will easily lose your camera balance. So I do not recommend you to do so. Just enjoy being naked in the nature like Japanese people enjoy hot spa bathing in the open air together with male and female without cameras.

This shot was taken before I fell into the water fall, so it is sharp and clear. In most cases I concentrate to one theme or subject and so the whole shots in a contact sheet are filled with the same subject with slight variations, but when I do not have a particular theme or subject I shoot at random, and my intuition orders me to pick up a shot out of the arbitrary shots. This often gives a very good photograph.

EIKOH HOSOE

21ˢᵗ JULY    PENARTH (Donkey Derby) WALES.

9A–28A    Man in Stocks having flour bags
          thrown at him.

22ⁿᵈ JULY    32A —  ROYAL SHOW  BUILTH WELLS.

255

DAVID HURN

The making of a perfect contact sheet from a processed film is vitally important. By "perfect" I mean that it must be as sharp as technically possible (which usually means ensuring flat, even contact between negatives and paper) and correctly exposed and printed. A fuzzy, unclean contact sheet is useless; a correctly made group of contact prints is one of the photographer's most useful tools.

The contact sheet is so important because it is the first time that you actually see a picture as opposed to reality. The image is now static and there is all the time in the world to make choices. You stand or fall by how critical you are with your own work and by the decisions that are made from a careful analysis of the contact sheet. The emotional involvements with the event at the time of shooting are now in the past. It is time for a cold, critical and objective appraisal of the image itself.

The contact sheet reveals how I have been thinking, and how efficiently my instincts have controlled the framing of the subject. If I have trained myself to deal with the small size, it also reaches me by revealing my mistakes without the expense of making enlargements. I can analyze each frame by asking myself such questions as: would the image have been better if I had moved a few feet to the left or right; could I have improved the picture by moving closer or further back; what would have been the result of releasing the shutter a second earlier, or later? Such ruthless self-examination through a contact sheet is one of the best teaching methods.

For me, the contact sheet has four main purposes:

1) I shoot a lot of what I call "dear diary" pictures. Those images have no foreseeable use and I never intend to enlarge them. But they act as simple visual records, personal reminders of people met and places visited. I will also shoot a frame of a street sign, to give me the location of other frames on the same roll of film. It's easier than writing down the information in a notebook.

One of the photographer's greatest pleasures is to look back at 10 year old contact sheets. The images provide an open door and total recall to the pleasures (and pains) of the past.

2) The contact sheet is a valuable teacher. Presumably, when a photographer presses the button it is because he believes the image is worthwhile. It rarely is. Why? If the photographer is self-critical he can attempt to analyse the reasons for the gap between expectation and actuality. This is a most effective learning process.

3) Marking the contact sheet isolates any particular frame in order that the image can be retrieved more quickly. It is a convenient time and money-saver. I use a different marking system (various colors of pencil) to identify the various uses of the photograph, whether magazine, exhibition print or personal gift. I also write on a large white area on the contact sheet, masked specifically for this purpose, and make notes to myself. These notes not only include a numbering system, and short captions of event, person or location, but also remind me that the picture should be reshot at a later date.

4) Looking at the contact sheets of other photographers' work allows me to understand their method of working and their thinking process. I gain an understanding, and often respect, of their final prints by this analysis.

In the contact sheet, reproduced here, are several frames from an event at a Donkey Derby in Wales. I saw the man in the stocks reacting to flour bags thrown at him by the public. I chose a viewpoint where I could clearly see his involvement in the action but also where a few spectators could be included. In this type of photography timing is crucial. It is impossible to predict the exact appearance of the image at the fraction of a second the shutter is open. There are too many randomly moving elements in the frame. It is important to shoot several frames in order to increase the chances that one of them will be "good", in the sense that all aspects of the flux are contributing to, and not distracting from, the final effect. For example, even though every other element might be just right, one of the spectators could have been looking at the camera. In this particular case, that would have been a distraction. In the end, frame No. 17 was selected for printing. The "victim" is caught at the right moment, the elements in the picture are balanced, and the group of spectators are contributing towards the picture's mood.

DAVID HURN

SEAN KERNAN

The best photographs that I have ever taken have
come to me so cleanly and effortlessly that I think of
them as having slipped past my labored search for
images.

I was wandering around the yard at the West
Virginia Penitentiary. There was an old heating plant
that was in the process of being torn down. There
was violence about it, like a war derelict.

On the edge of this place there was a steam vent
blowing white into the early winter air, and not far
away there was a grizzled convict playing with a
kitten. I took a few frames where he stood, then
asked him to move near the steam.

Now, after the fact, the steam seems like a crescent
of purity cut into the midst of this devastation. At the
time I thought more of the lines in Francis Bacon's
paintings that seem to focus the energy, and also of
the white cloths that itinerant photographers used to
hang behind their subjects.

These thoughts were in my head at the time. They
have little to do with how things turned out. I think
the picture is of a moment when everything
touched—the light, the lives, the violence and the
tenderness. I had about enough presence to
remember to use the camera.

Technically, the picture was made with the 28mm
lens I usually use, and shot on Tri-X. The print is
heavily burned on the left side, then rubbed with hot
developer to take that area down.

SEAN KERNAN

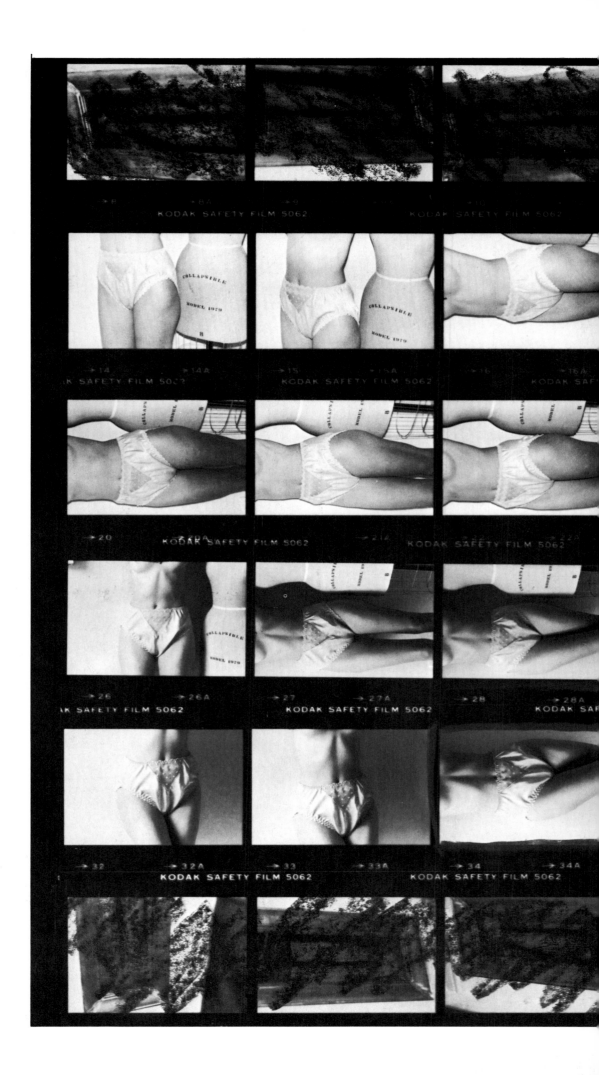

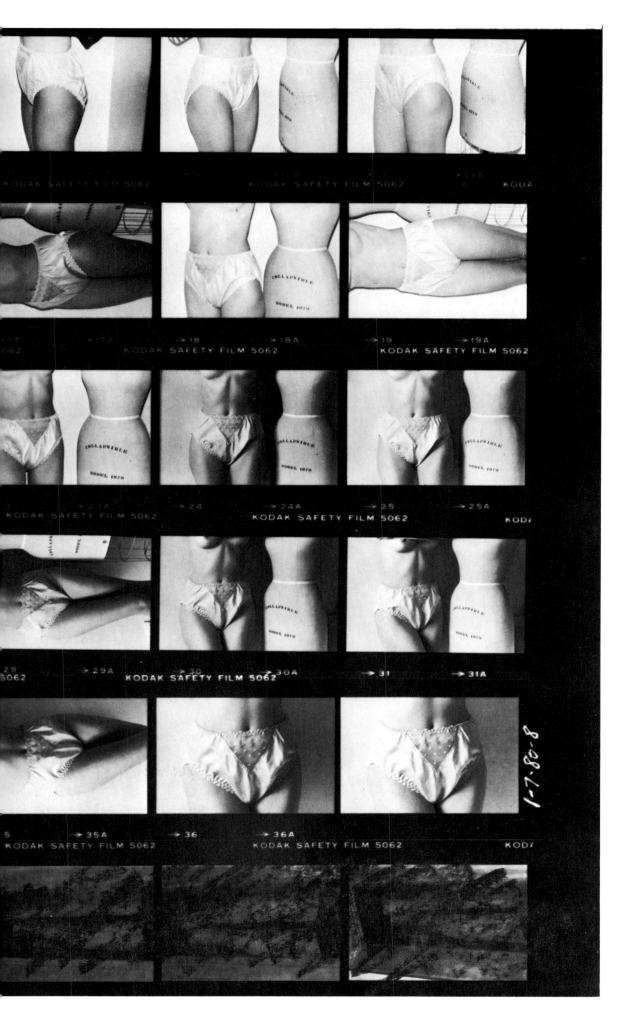

ALAN LEWIS KLEINBERG

For me, this contact sheet contains only 14 frames...
It serves to confirm a series of realizations and
decisions that took place during a shooting.

The underpants were one of several items I was
assigned to photograph. I had photographed
everything except a pair of shoes that didn't fit the
professional model, Patti, who worked with me on
the shooting. A friend, who I'll call Shy, with the right
shoe size, agreed to stand in for the stocking and shoe
picture. Frames 2-9 are the tail end of that picture, too
close, rejected.

We seemed to be finished with the entire shooting,
except, I had a gnawing feeling that the picture of the
underpants hadn't worked. We had pinned them,
stretching and flattening them to look better on Patti's
trim boyish figure. The picture still lacked something,
hoping to give the picture more punch I decided to
use a mixture of daylight and flash.

Still uncomfortable with the picture I had taken, I
convinced Shy to try on the underpants. The
roundness of Shy's body changed the picture, pinning
wasn't necessary. I liked the way they looked, puffy
and bulging like that, I decided to reshoot them.

Forgeting I had only used the flash to compensate
for a problem I had with the underpants on Patti, it
took 13 frames for me to realize the fullness of Shy's
figure, the available light and the underpants all
worked together—the flash was working against me.

The 24th frame begins my 14 frames of choice.
Moving around her trying to find a point of view, it
took a few exposures for me to realize that I wasn't
helping Shy, she looked stiff. I asked her to shift her
position slightly, once that happens (frame 28) I begin
to find the photograph I want. The mannequin
becomes superfluous, the photograph becomes a
figure study instead of a picture of a pair of
underpants alongside a clever prop.

Frame 34, published in the layout, has the
cropping, the light and the attitude I originally
wanted...

ALAN LEWIS KLEINBERG

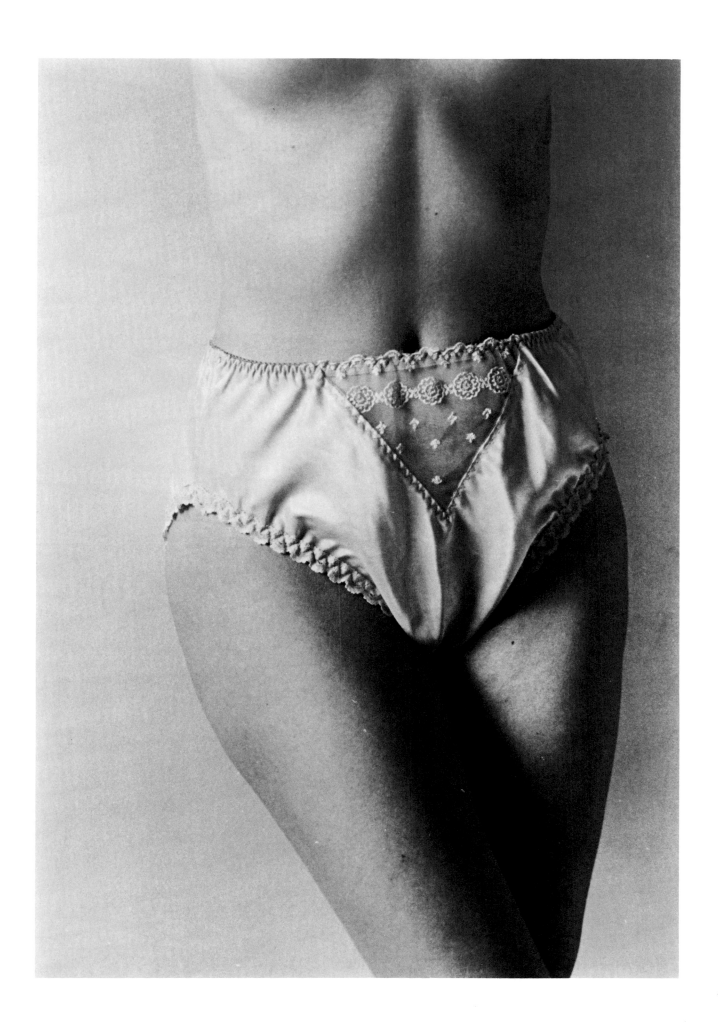

GEORGE KRAUSE

There was a time when I worked long and hard to make beautifully printed contact sheets. I still encourage others to take their time and get the most out of the negative when printing their contacts. It now matters little to me that the contact print is too dark (rather too dark than too light as I prefer to view my contacts on a light table) or that there may be scratches on the glass in the contact printer. I've become impatient and contact sheets are now necessary only as a brief first stage in the editing of my work. While contacts are convenient for examining the progress of an idea during photographing, the importance they play in the editing and understanding of my ideas has been replaced by what I call "sketch prints." These sketch prints can be seen in the print I've selected for this article. The making of contacts is still a most exciting and magical step in the process of finishing a photograph. I first anxiously look over the wet contact sheets. (I don't imagine I will ever approach this initial stage calmly or patiently.) Once dried, I again look over them marking with a yellow grease pencil those that seem promising. With mixed emotions (disappointed and excited with what they have shown me) I put the contact sheets away for a few days, allowing the first impressions (after image) to form. Later, in a calm and self controlled state I attack them for a third time and at this point I often discover images missed completely in the earlier viewing. These overlooked images I now mark in red grease pencil. I then cut the contacts sheets into strips and fasten them onto the negative envelope containing the corresponding negative. This is my filing system. Those contact strips/negatives that I understand completely and hold no beauty or mystery for me I throw away. The remaining contacts/negatives are divided into two piles—those I understand and like and those I don't. Many of my strongest images come from the second group. Once the initial editing has been done, because there is a kaleidoscopic charm/danger inherent in a contact sheet, I have to isolate the individual image from the others on the contact sheet. While printing the sketch prints I may find still others on the contact sheet that surprise me. The sketch prints are then placed on my wall to study and live with for awhile. I have evolved this editing process to help me to better understand my work and know how to put my thoughts and ideas into the final print. It is a complex process and often takes many years.

GEORGE KRAUSE

ERICA LENNARD

Contact sheets represent a very personal kind of vocabulary. Just as the film director looks at his rushes or the architect deciphers his plans, there is a long way to go from the photograph that was shot and the final print. Because I do both personal work and assignments, (fashion and portraits) I have come to appreciate the luxury of being able to sit down with my own contact sheet of a particular project and decide slowly which images I shall print. After reading the contact sheet I decide to print only the images that I strongly believe will represent what I am pursuing at the time of the project. I suppose that comes through years of experience and each photographer learns to be more familiar with his or her language. If I give my work to an art director on a commercial assignment having already made my choices, they will rarely be able to show me an image I did not already see, nor choose as a successful photo one I didn't indicate.

This contact sheet is from a recent project on gardens and looking at it is always a pleasure because, like an anecdote, it reminds me of the actual visual promenade that very cold day in the Parc de Sceaux outside of Paris. I suppose that as I walked about in these various places it was the moment of first sighting something that made the strongest impact. Because by nature the subject does not move I could have shot each image in a million different ways but as you can see some of my most successful pictures were recorded in a unique frame. I always like to wait a week or two after the actual shooting before beginning to decipher and choose the images I wish to print. I need that distance to clarify or extract those essential feelings.

There is no real formula in choosing. Intuition plays a very great role. Often I find that if I go back to contact sheets that are very old my personal vision has evolved and I tend to see entirely new things. But rather than looking at old contacts (which always make me very nostalgic) I prefer to shoot new pictures.

There were three images from this sheet I chose to include in my exhibition in New York and in the book I am preparing on gardens. The frame 26-26a was the first one I chose. It struck me as a transformation or modernization of a very traditional french park. I suppose I was thinking a lot about scale and maybe this giant cube had an "other worldly" quality. The other two images reflect strongly the very arid and abandoned feeling I had in this place. In the image 13-13a, the people seen at a distance serve to increase the proportions of those strange conical trees. I would usually wait however, till the few people in the park were gone. In my garden pictures, unless the people are photographed at a great distance they tend to destroy the mystery of the place by explaining immediately the scale and by designating the era. I shot many of these trees but in this frame the trees appeared highly separated from their background.

The final picture of the pond, 33-33a also has an "other worldly" quality: one of those strangely floating modern shapes with a horizon that continues on into infinity. I darken the skies considerably in the final prints and diffuse them as I do in most of my photographs. It seems to add another dimension to the blacks, gives them more depth and makes the overall print more luminous. When they are finally printed the photographs do speak for themselves.

ERICA LENNARD

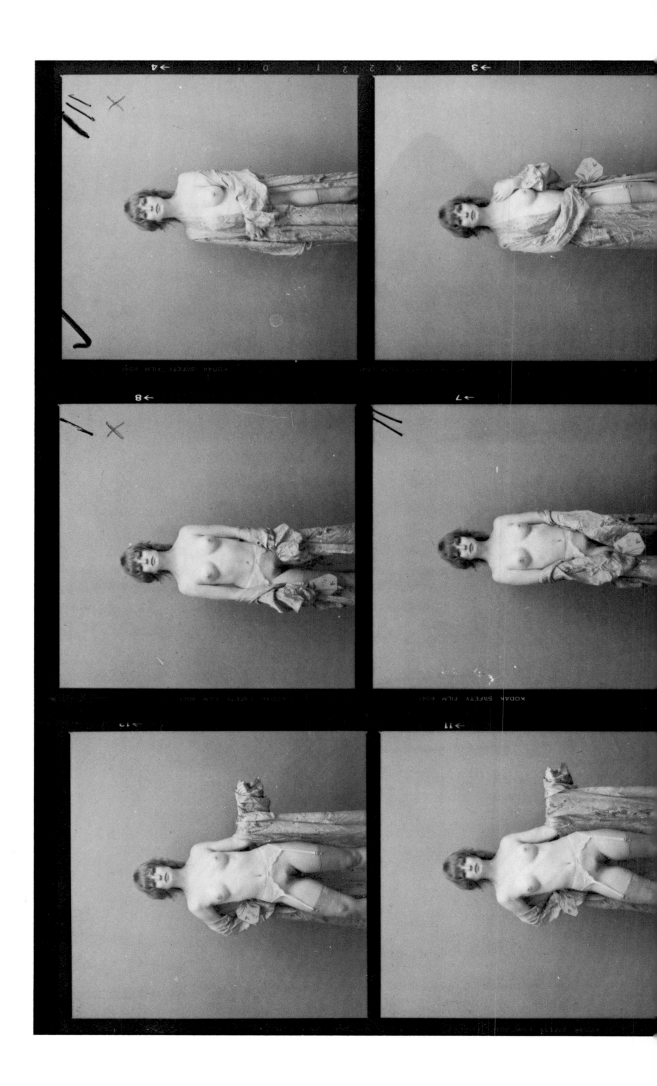

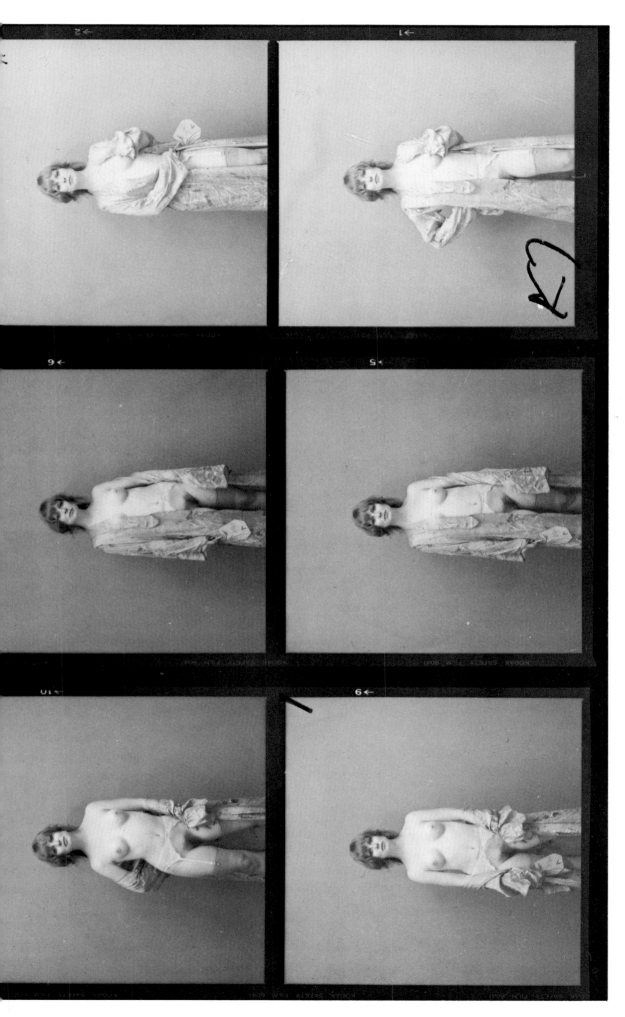

ARNE LEWIS

Years ago as a little kid I spent Saturday afternoons at the Art Students League in New York. I'd stand resolutely at an easel with a box of vine charcoal making endless drawings of nude models. Occasionally something recognizable would happen on the surface of the white charcoal paper. At the end of the day I'd trundle back to Harlem on the A train covered with charcoal dust, my portfolio of the days work under my arm. Thirty years later I've come full circle. Memories of early development prompted this project "Anonymous Portraits."

I chose to print frame No. 10 from this contact sheet because I was persuaded by its charm and vulnerability. I love the line of the hip and the opposing arm softened by feminine drapery. Shades of art school days! The photographic print is more mysterious and satisfying because the image is fused in the emulsion. To select from the shooting I project the contact sheet using an old 8 x 10 opaque projector. Seeing the frames in this way speeds up the point at which intuition and memory cross. My prints are light in tone because I am stingy with dense blacks. The interplay of light and shadow, on and in the figure, and its interaction with the gray mass behind fascinates me endlessly. I am hopelessly in love with all the colors and overtones of gray.

TECHNICAL NOTES: SL-66 camera, S-Planar 1:5.6 120mm lens, Plus-X film, rated normal. Rodinal developer, 68 F, 18cc's per roll, 14½ minutes, 15 seconds agitation every minute, tank inversion method. Omega D2 enlarger, 75mm Rodenstock Omegaron lens, 213 bulb. Usual aperture f/16 for 13½ seconds. Brovira 111, 16 x 20, No 1, developed in TST, 225 cc's Solution A, 15cc's Solution B, developed for 3 minutes. Image area 13⅞ x 13⅞, even border top, left and right. 20 seconds in 28% glacial acetic acid solution, 2 baths Rapid Fix, 3½ minutes each. 5 minutes wash in very warm water, 5 minutes in very hot* combined solution, 3 oz hypo eliminator, 6 oz selenium toner*. 40 minutes final hand wash, air dry on fiberglass screens. Prints are flattened in dry mount press, unmounted, signed in very hard pencil on verso.

---

*Not recommended by the manufacturer. Hot water produces a dull enamel surface on Brovira 111, both subtle and beautiful.

ARNE LEWIS

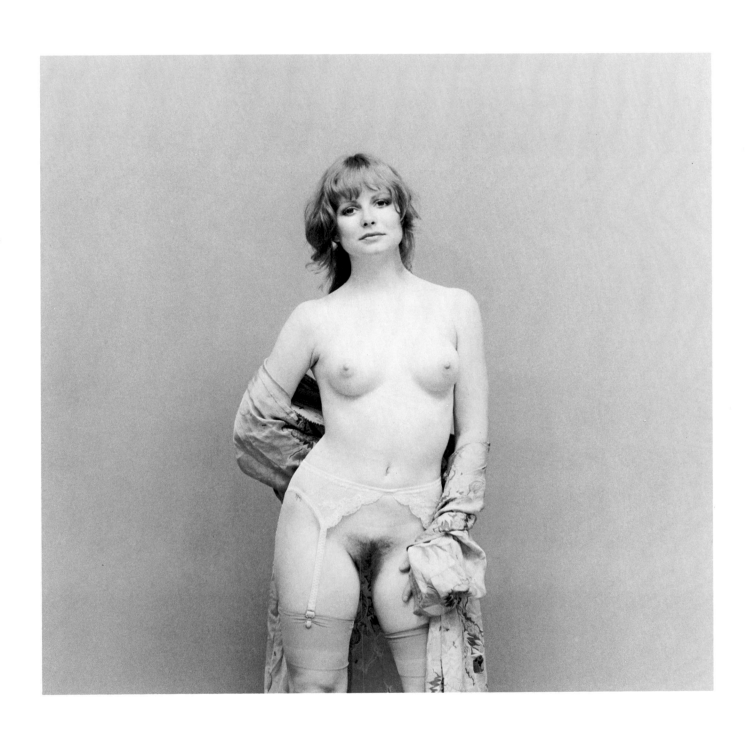

JOAN LIFTIN

I was in Paris for a few weeks working in an office and found myself getting itchy about not being able to get out and photograph. So I took off very early one morning for Versailles and arrived a couple of hours before other visitors. I wanted to see the place as Atget had, without any people.

The grounds were very quiet. Working in such silence seemed to reduce much of the tension I often feel while photographing and I think I became rather sedated. The one moment of surprise came when I was photographing the statue of a woman (frame 8a) and suddenly noticed the rooster crouching under her robe. The shock of seeing that animal and feeling its fear in what had up to then been such a benign, calm place probably accounts for the picture's intensity, and is why I edited it. All the other pictures I took that morning seem to be "under glass" much like the gardens appeared to me at first.

JOAN LIFTIN

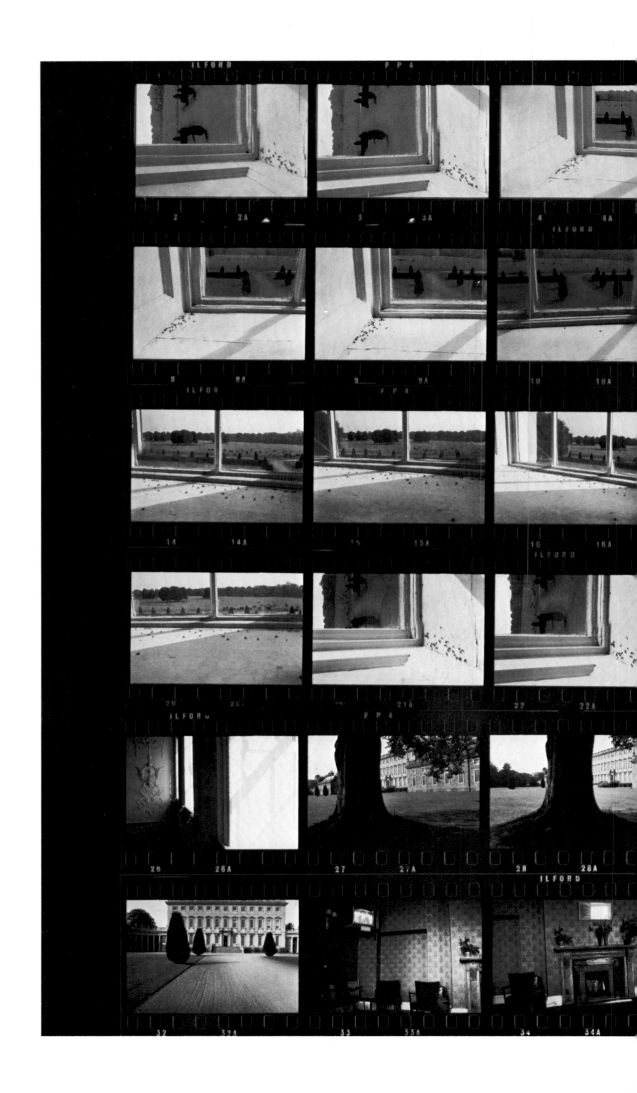

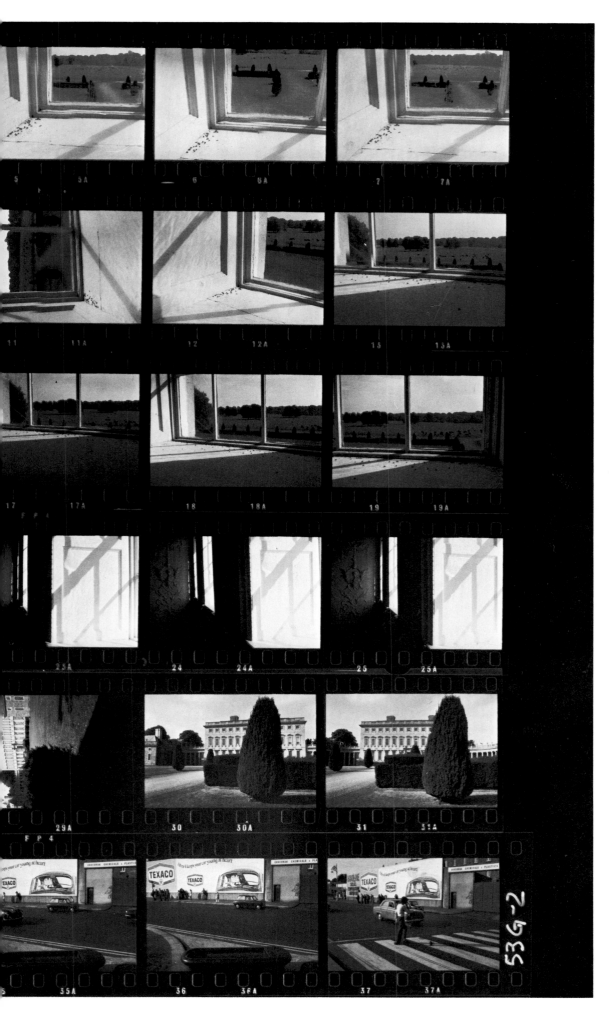

ALEN MACWEENEY

I'd love to write something about the process of editing contacts. I find it difficult and interesting, and rather like a child who, having fallen into the water, swims whatever way it can to safety; my predicament is also the unknown, and the shore is my aim too. The illusion, or the idea, of having taken an exciting photograph is a burden, stirring up nervousness, excessive interest, and generally unbalancing one's readiness to make a selection from what is on the contact sheet, rather than what is in the mind.

Adopting the posture of an analyst I examine the contact sheets with a mixture of some entertainment and remove, trying to maintain enough distance to enjoy them. Nonetheless emotions threaten the calm; spirits vacillate and the original picture in the mind's eye fades. Self-realizations of an unpleasant sort surface rapidly. Still suspending decision and with a kind of savage persistence the examination continues, backwards and forwards, until finally either there're a few irrefutable survivors, or nothing left but dust.

Of these final selections I make small rough prints. I regard them, still at a purposeful remove, like a stranger looking in through a window. I think I wait for the picture to initiate the conversation and invite me in, whereupon I feel the warmth of some re-kindled enthusiasm. There are other times when there's nothing felt at all. I leave these mute prints lying around for a while, looking at them now and again. If something in one still makes itself felt to me, seems to have persistence equal to my own. I'll make a good print of it too.

That's my pattern today; tomorrow may be different. And as with any true act of expression, photographic selection defies system, methods, and definition, and is as immeasurably indifferent to such struggles as the sea.

ALEN MACWEENEY

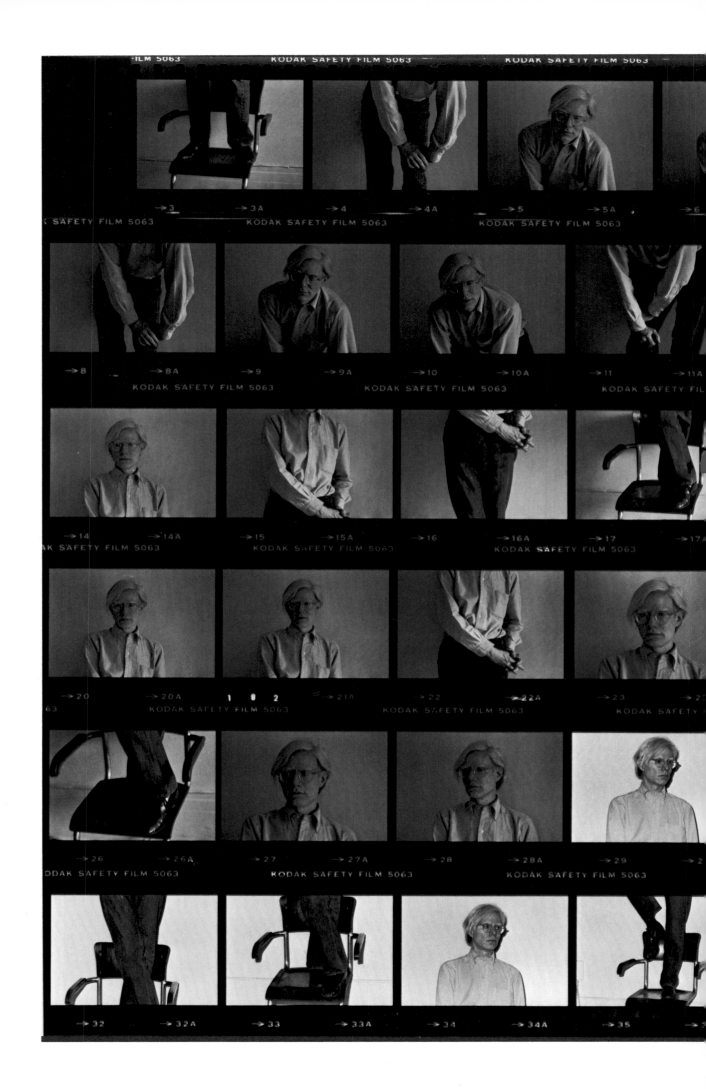

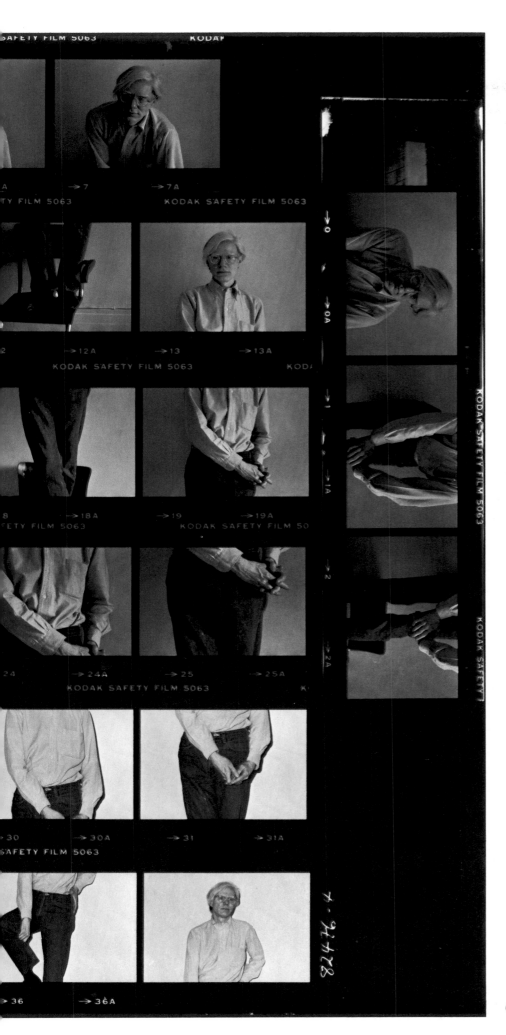

CHRISTOPHER MAKOS

Hollywood, 1980, The Contact Sheet and Me

Klaus Moser develops my contact sheets, the only
part of the photographic process that I'm not directly
involved with. I'm quite removed from my contacts
until I need to look at the individual frames to make a
SECTION portrait. It takes a few months of
investigating the contact sheet to arrive at a finished
SECTION portrait. As editor-in-chief of my own work
it is my job to take the contact information and piece
it together into a SECTION portrait. Here the contacts
find their genre. The SECTION portraits came about
from the investigation of the negative and led to the
breaking apart of the single image photograph in my
work. After years of looking at photographs in
magazines, books, movies and all other single image
media it just seemed natural to play with the negative
as a response to the 36 images on the contact. After
all, the contact sheet is one whole image sectioned
into 36 pieces.

   The process of going from contact to blow up, 36 to
3 or 4, to one over all image is unique to my
B & W work. I edit my color with a slide projector,
viewing the individual images as singular and whole.
The contact sheet has lost its genre in this editing
process, as evidenced by the absence of sectioned
images in my color work.

CHRISTOPHER MAKOS

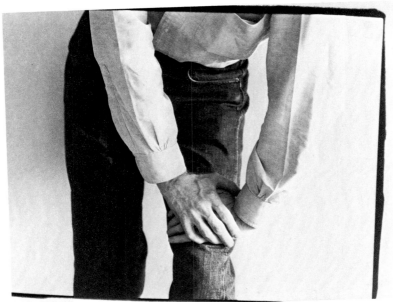

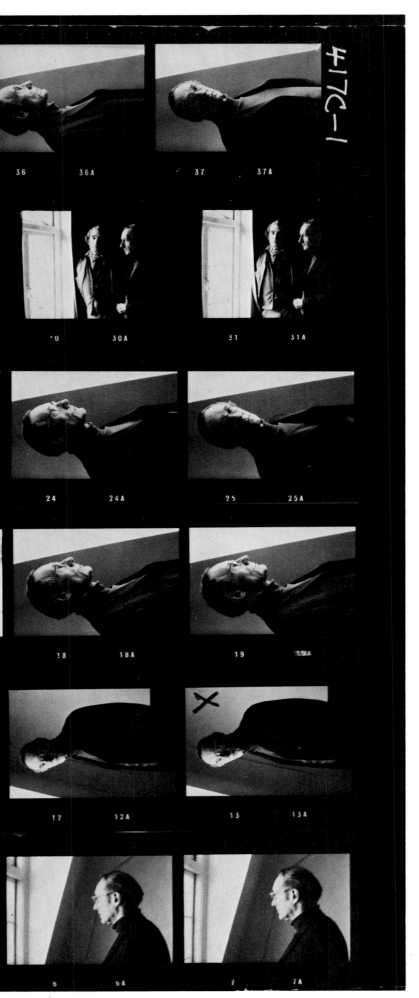

GERARD MALANGA

Demystifying The Appearance of the Real or
William Burroughs: Male Model. 15/15A

A contact-sheet could be termed the sequential
authentication or dramatization of what the
photographer makes in the space of time allotted him
during a given occasion. It is a sequential
enumeration of emotive similitude. The contact-sheet
is evidence of the photographer's subjective
perception of an occasion which constitutes a series of
sequence of seized moments. The contact-sheet of
these seized moments exists outside a stated piece of
time and yet re-invents time by recording it as a
referential to visual notation.

I read a contact-sheet in such a way that what is
sequential in the world of physical existence is
recorded visual experience derived from it. I select
the single frame which will represent the subject or
occasion under my scrutiny, stripping away all the
"misses", i.e., a cropped jacket pocket-flap or part of
the hand, the finger. Taken as a whole, all the contact
frames are the picture-units of experience. When I
examine contacts of a shooting session or occasion, I
am amazed at the range of the subtle changes of
expression: slight tilts of the head, the variety of
stances and body postures. The position of the head
or the eyes may evoke sadness or joy or ambiguity.
What the subject wears can be important in terms of
body tone.

Richard Nixon, the first U.S. President to fully utilize
the potential of the news media, once remarked: "a
camera can misquote or misinterpret a man. An
unconscious, unintentional upturning of the lips can
appear in a picture as a smile at a given moment. On
the other hand, too serious an expression could create
an impression of fear and concern which also would
be most unfortunate." What becomes evident is how
far the photographer's own implied character might
manipulate the situation to produce a subtle variant
on "reality" in a medium that's supposedly totally
honest about what it sees.

What the figure of a photo- or gestural-portrait
exists in is a space which has a floor, possibly a wall,
and a source of natural light. In other words, the
entire image—not just the person in the picture—has
a viewpoint which I try to convey. The subject simply
exists—stays in the frame as a solution of a formal
problem—as the possibility of a pictorial space or
environment. Whatever the subject is, is its
environment, e.g., William Burroughs in profile
staring at and through a window into another space.

I want to pull in as much visual experience and
information as possible into the moment of
perception represented by the picture. William stands
in a narrowly defined visual space: a room with a
window supposedly looking out into nothing and the
interior's background comprised of a blank wall.

We seemed to be walking around each other
without really looking at each other except when
occasionally I would put the camera to eye and shoot.
It was a silent experience. William never said a word
the entire time I was photographing him. He was not
posing when I made the picture of him looking at the
window. He, in a very direct sense, "gave" me the
picture. I like this picture because it doesn't unlock
any secrets or reveal anything about Burroughs the
writer. There is nothing imagined in his qualities.
Rather, William appears more anonymous, less
magnified than "William Burroughs." He looks like
someone who looks "famous" but isn't. The paradox.
So, in seeking the anonymous in someone famous, I
try emphasizing that quality. William brings attention
to the photograph without bringing attention to
himself. This is what I mean by the subject's "giving"
me the picture.

I think Burroughs has an innate understanding of
what a camera can and cannot do, as well as the
experience of having seen himself often in
photographs. For he is no stranger to being
photographed, having been frequently subjected to
photographers who wanted him to hold still for "just
one more!"

I am carefully making choices in the act of
photography: the moving-around-the-subject to seize
from it its several successive appearances. I'm literally
composing the shot with my eye thru the view-finder.
The finished print for me is an untouched, uncropped
image that matches my initial viewing experience of
looking through the lens and pressing the shutter. I'm
primarily concerned with the shapes of things that
make themselves evident around the subject in the
frame—not just the subject but the entire picture as
content and aesthetic/installation object.

I move toward a complexity in my work that makes
what I do the-picture-is-its-subject and which does not
necessarily (although it may) point to something other
than itself, as some viewers seem to think. The only
simplicity I want is that of a coherent thing and trust
that a result of integrity of the picture-as-a-whole will
come clear, finally, of any unrelated meanings that
would displace its validity. Susan Sontag, in ON
PHOTOGRAPHY, notes that events are "pieces of
evidence in an ongoing biography or history." History
as told or seen in photographs is viewed by me as a
process of turning what had been thought to be
inescapable limitations into human possibilities. In
that instance, then, my pictures are intended as
documentation of both biographical and
autobiographical data.

GERARD MALANGA

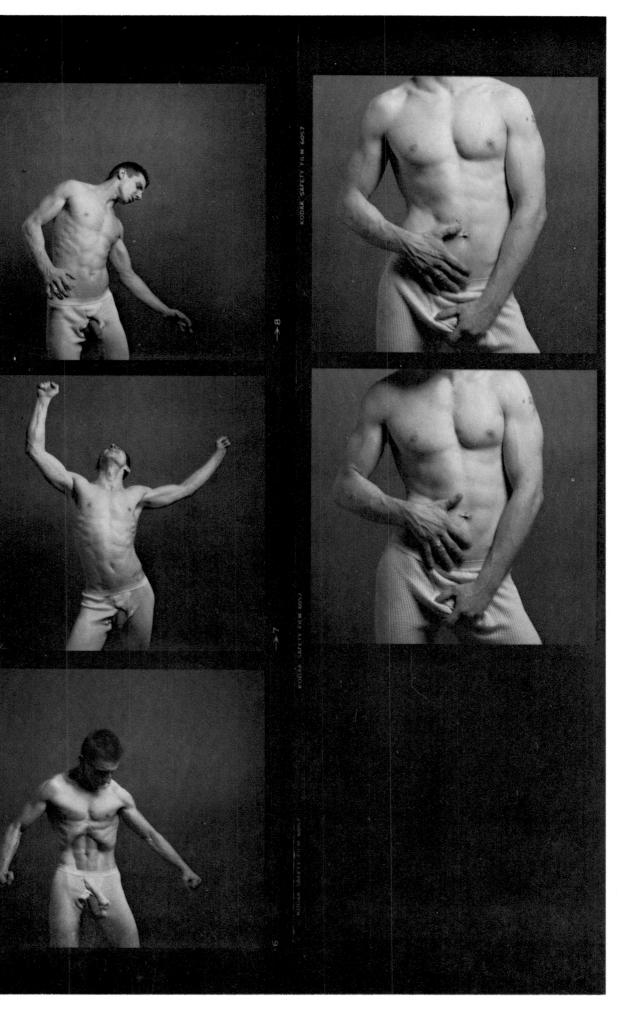

ROBERT MAPPLETHORPE

121

This sheet of contacts was taken on the aftermath of a rather stoned evening in New York. The camera was set up on a tripod and using a cable release, a sequence was taken—This is one contact sheet from that session which contains what I consider one of my more successful portraits. Tri-X film was used shot at 1/500 second at f/16 with a Hasselblad 80mm lens and strobe. On examination of this contact sheet I noticed a photo that interested me so I proceeded to have a 16 x 20 enlargement made. I realized that the facial expression was extraordinary enough for me to attempt to come in on just this aspect of the photograph. At this same period in time I had been experimenting with my printer and working with the possibilities of printing very dark. We decided to attempt this portrait on a scale of dark gray to black. The following was the result.

ROBERT MAPPLETHORPE

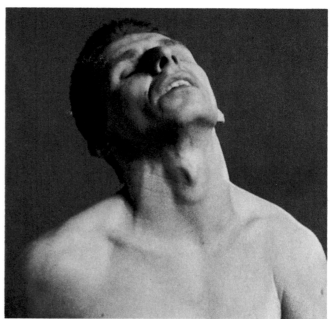

124

MARY ELLEN MARK

Frame No. 22-A is the photograph that finally became the cover for my book WARD 81 —frames No. 20, 21A and 23A and 19A are quite similar—

Frames No. 19-A and 21A were eliminated because of the plain shirt in the right side of the frame— sometimes disturbing elements like this can be eliminated by trimming the side of the frame (although most of the time I hate to crop pictures). In this case if I trimmed the side of the photograph it would have destroyed my frame—it is very important that the right side of the bath tub hits the right corner of the frame exactly the way it does if I trimmed the right side this would be impossible—there is too much coat showing.

Frames No. 21A, 22A and 23A are almost exactly alike—I picked frame 22A because I liked the expression in her eyes the best—in frame 21A I did not like her left eye—Laurie has a loose muscle in her left eye—in frame 23A I felt her gaze was not concentrated enough on me also again her left eye bothered me—in frame 22A her attention was fixed on the camera it just seemed right to me—

In reviewing this contact sheet I just re-noticed frame 24A—I think I'm going to make a print of it. This sometimes happens when you stay away from your contacts for a long time (I have not edited this sheet for three years). You will often go back and find very good pictures that you missed before—I think often the distance of both emotions and time can give you a fresh perspective on your contact sheets.

MARY ELLEN MARK

RAY MORTENSON

Given time, peace of mind, and the right attitude, looking through contact sheets can be as exciting as looking through the camera itself. Far from being just a simple step between exposure and final print, the contacts are the beginning of a long and complex struggle. Indeed, for me, this is the most important, most frustrating and usually most rewarding challenge I face in my work.

I look through the contacts for the first time only after they are washed, dried and flattened. To select at this point is premature. I even find that having a marking pencil is an annoyance. I merely try to acquaint myself with what I saw through the camera. After this first look, it is best to put the sheets aside, keeping an open mind and avoiding a rapid choice.

I return for a second look a day or two later. Using the pencil this time, I mark every frame that seems interesting enough to deserve a closer look. For me, this is usually three to six frames per fifteen exposure roll; in the sheet shown here, I chose three frames. Next I enlarge each selected frame into a small (5″×7″) print. I work quickly and mechanically. Basically I am making a second contact—one that is enlarged, edited and separated into a single frame.

Now I can begin to see and judge the work clearly. Lifted from the initial sheet, the separate identity of each enlarged frame emerges and the image becomes visually accessible. It can be picked up, moved around and examined with ease, allowing me the freedom I need to shape the work.

I keep these prints around, stacked in different piles, and spend a lot of time editing them in and out of "yes," "no" and "maybe" piles. I return to them often, constantly reviewing and re-editing—until finally the strongest prints survive the process and evolve into the work itself. I selected the shot of the man fishing from the bridge, for instance, because the strong contrast of the human figure against the surrounding industrial and organic landscape held my attention.

Even while writing this, however, I feel renewed interest in the frame of the bridge roadbed in the extreme lower left of the sheet. The process is never really over. Clearly the eye can and does learn. Going all the way back once more to the initial contact sheet, seeing what I may have missed before, gives me insight into what I have done and often points me toward new work.

RAY MORTENSON

HANS NAMUTH

133

Contact No. 141/1950/Jackson Pollock

Contact is what a group of negatives leaves on a piece of photographic paper. It is also an all-important key to the final print.

Some people are geniuses at reading a contact sheet. Others are blind. I remember bringing back a few dozen contacts from an assignment for HARPERS BAZAAR and showing them to the art director, Alexey Brodovitch. It was a story about five painters of eastern Long Island. It took him seconds to look at one sheet, minutes to scan the lot, making marks with his grease pencil here and there (very few) and handing them back to me. "Very good, Hans." (Elation.) It resulted in a five-page story.

Brodovitch never missed—it amazed and startled me each time. With an eagle eye he could spot the exact picture frame on a given sheet containing 36 or 12 exposures which could range from medium fair to excellent.

I can truly say Brodovitch taught me to read… He taught me how to read contact prints.

Pollock contact sheet No. 133 to 144 contains several usable exposures. That makes it more difficult to choose the one— if there is one to be chosen.

The pictures were part of a series taken over a number of weekends during the summer of 1950, one of Jackson Pollock's great creative and most productive periods. We had established by then a relationship of trust and confidence in each other. At times he would wait for my arrival in Springs, Easthampton, to continue or to start an important work. We did not spell it out at the time but our unspoken aim was to put together a series of photographs, a record of his working methods. This sheet testifies to the extraordinary intimacy of our relationship.

I was to select the most significant shot from twelve suitable for a cover. I thought nothing of cropping a square picture then; that is precisely why I had been drawn to the Rolleiflex format; a 2¼ x 2¼ can easily become a horizontal or a vertical.

The following frames were under scrutiny: No. 135; 138; 141; 142 and 143. No. 141 won out because it was different from any other shot of Pollock taken up to that time. The beam of sunlight, already visible in No. 136, had just struck Pollock during his frenetic dance around the canvas. The slow shutter speed (1/25? 1/50? who knows!) gave the figure a ghostlike appearance. For a fleeting moment the painter himself was to become an abstraction.

It was apparent even then that the painting on the floor was an important one—one of the three, four truly great Pollocks. It is called "Autumn Rhythm" (No. 30, 1950) and was chosen by Robert Hale in 1957 to become part of the permanent collection of the Metropolitan Museum in New York where it can be seen to this day.

HANS NAMUTH

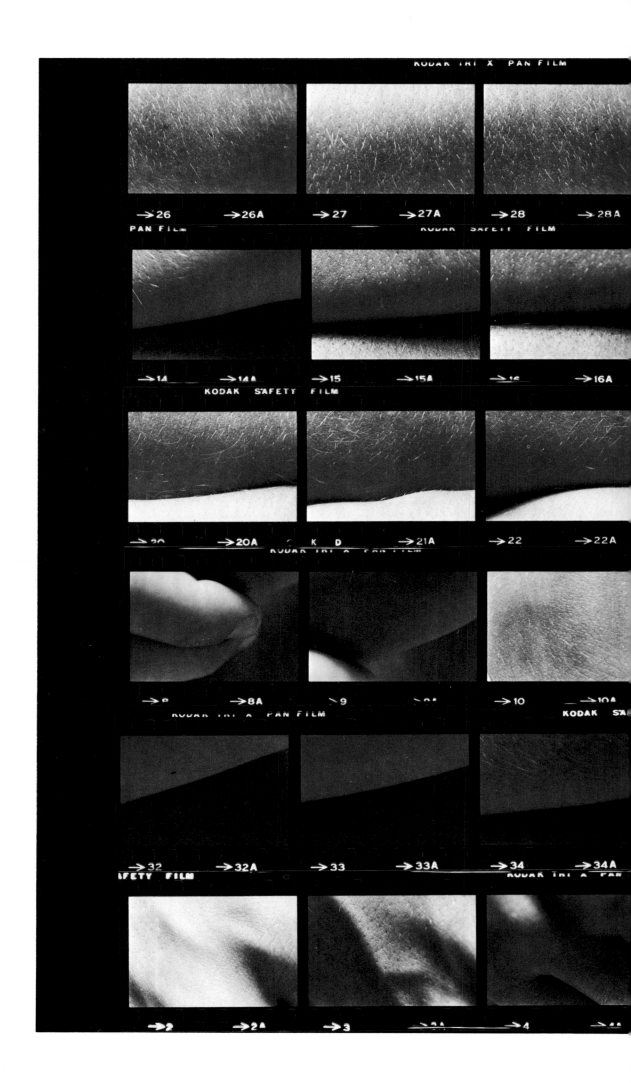

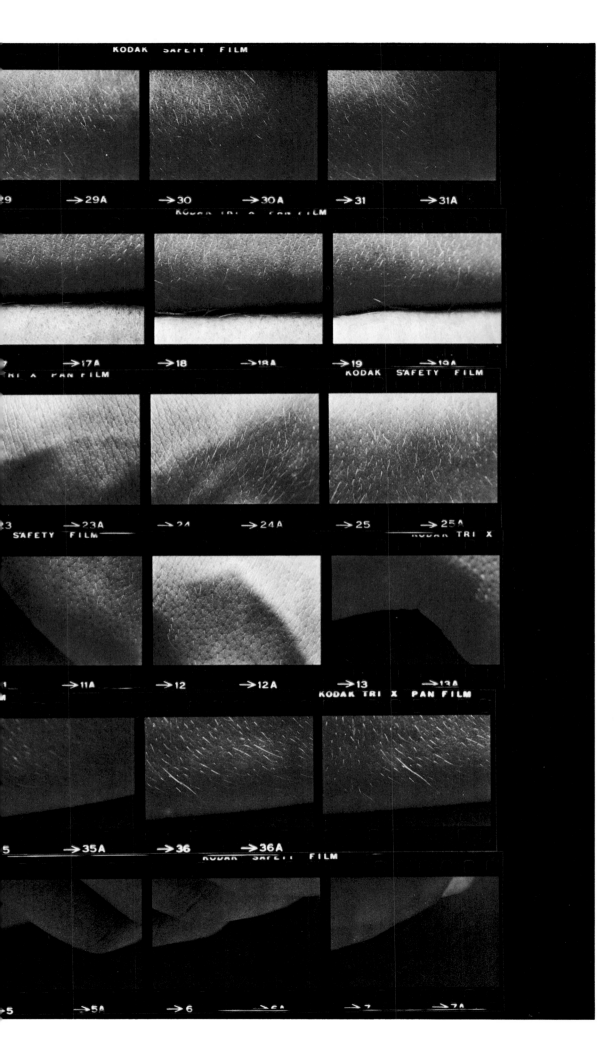

TETSU OKUHARA

*Title: Woman With Crossed Arms
Size: 36″ Square (Framed)
Date: 1973 NYC

The white rectangles separated by grids and underlined by letters and numbers floating on black are very beautiful. They are little windows offering private views of the world. Each of these windows demands a closer look.

I begin with an image in my mind, then I make sketches. If I feel the work is going well, I take a few photographs and assemble a simplified photographic model of the image I am trying to create. I often use thousands of images. The one published here is put together from 336 separate negatives. Some are repeated. Hundreds more are discarded.

After taking the photographs; I contact print the negatives, cut them out of the contact sheets and begin assembling them. This process is sometimes tedious but more often the shooting, processing, printing, cutting, and assembling—followed by more shooting, processing, etc.—I find pleasurable and in someways almost meditative.

*IN THE WITKIN GALLERY

TETSU OKUHARA

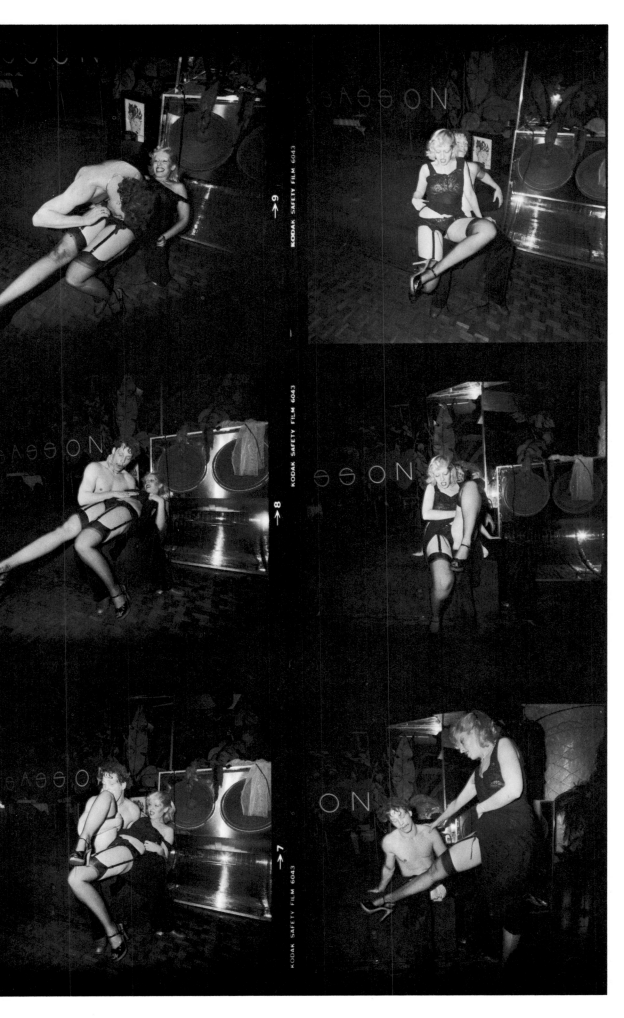

TOBY OLD

Contact

For the past three years my main focus has been on the disco party scene in New York City. My aim has been to document a particular scene at a certain period in history. Working this way enables me to go back to the same or different clubs on numerous occasions to observe and to make a personal record of the experience.

The manner in which I select images from my contact sheets might best be examined by describing the method in which I work. After each shooting or series of shootings I process the film and make contact sheets. Upon examination, certain images are selected from which I make work prints that are usually eleven by fourteen inches in size. These prints are put up on my work board for me to study and live with. If the image lasts I make a sixteen by twenty print of it which I feel is the best size for exhibition.

Since I am working on a series, the final body of work is dependent on a coherent theme. It is important that there be an interrelationship between images. Through this process—negative, contact sheet, work print, I determine and select images for final prints. It is also important to me that each image work as a singular image as well as within the context of the series.

Contact sheets contain certain clues which may serve as a catalyst for a particular idea. The idea then ferments in my mind and allows me to focus my attention on a specific project. The particular image reproduced here was chosen because I felt it demonstrated the strongest communication between the subject, Gypsy, and myself. In the others the gestures are more elusive or simply don't work visually due to distracting background elements. I try to select the strongest image that works on as many levels as possible.

TOBY OLD

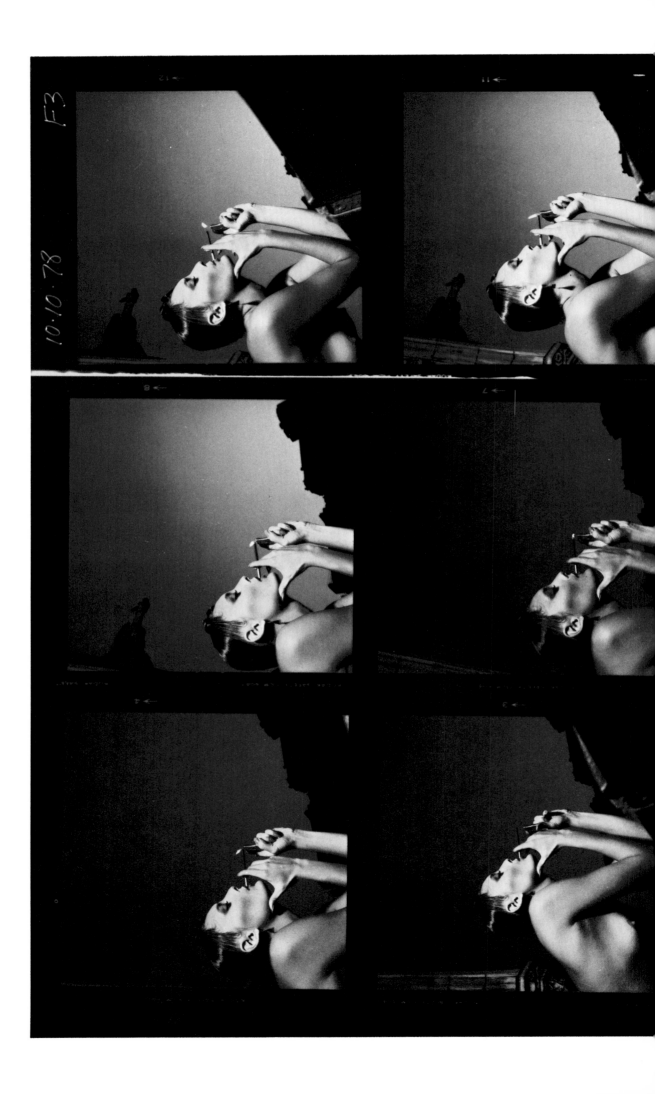

144

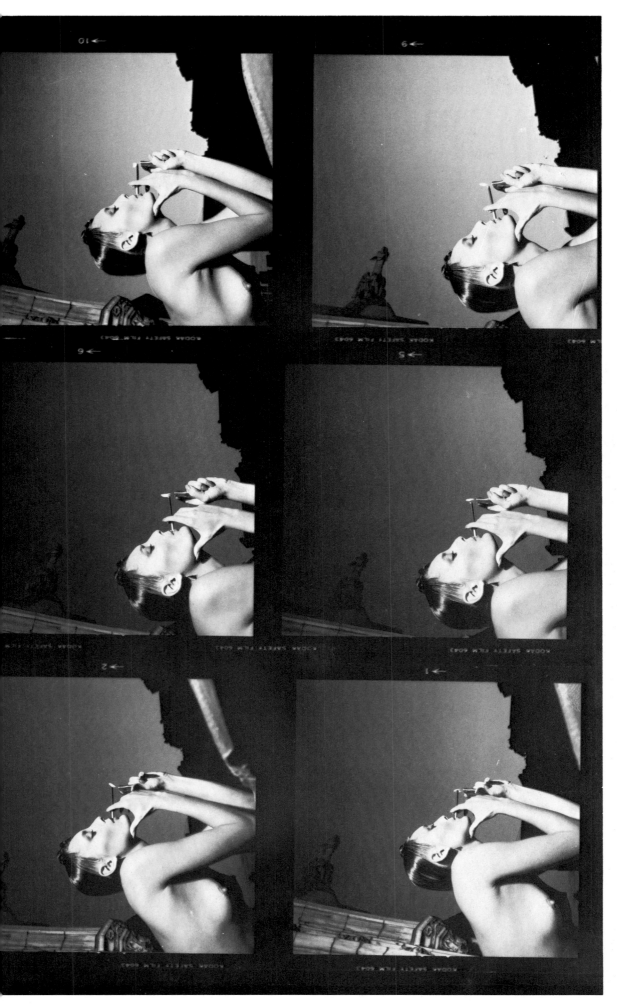

JEAN PAGLIUSO

Because I was first a layout artist before becoming a photographer, I go about a shooting in a different way. First I begin with little drawings of ideas, keeping the amount of pages and their sequence in mind. After the shooting session I then use the contacts in much the same manner as my drawings placing them in order sequentially. I make two or three copies from each take, then I make a little booklet of them. By juxtaposing one next to the other, I am able to make the best choice for the context of the article. This process adds to a new sense of balance and dynamics in the finished portfolio.

And this brings me to another point. By carefully indicating the choice and framing on each contact sheet, I can make a influential suggestion to the art director or editor.

Contact sheets are permanent records. Three years from now I may extract an "out-take" which will now become the focus of a new theme or a new approach. For each photograph, the shape of the subject in front of me sort of finds a place within the frame. I solidify my choice in the polaroid and make very subtle changes in what I see.

In this case, the final choice was determined by the quality of light, the framing of the subject and the clarity of the merchandise.

JEAN PAGLIUSO

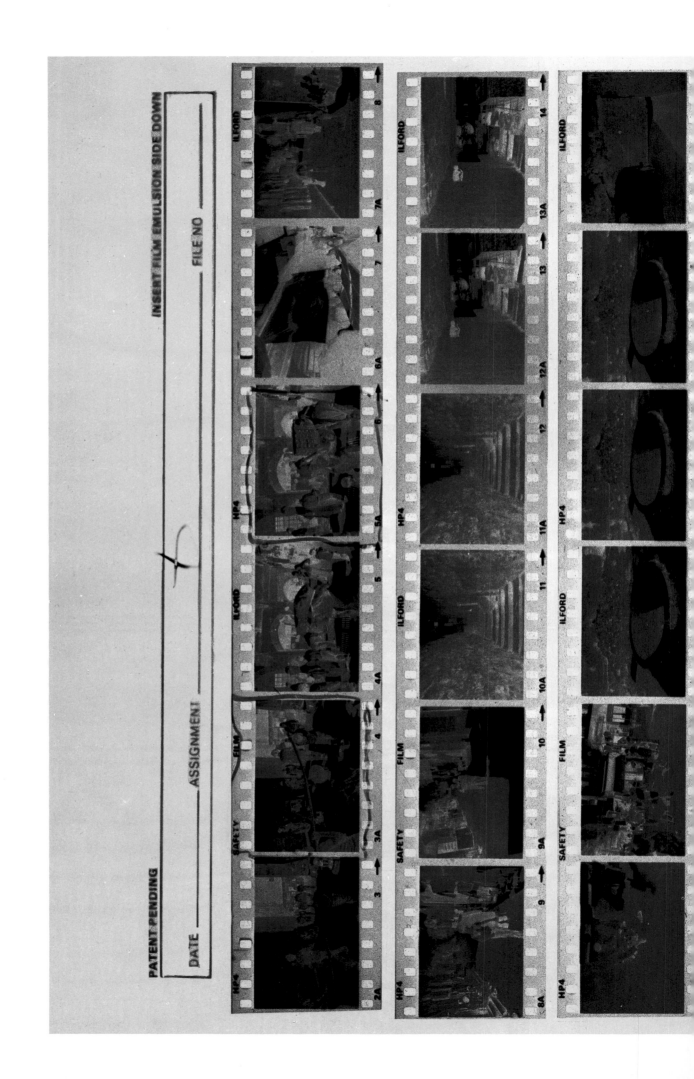

148

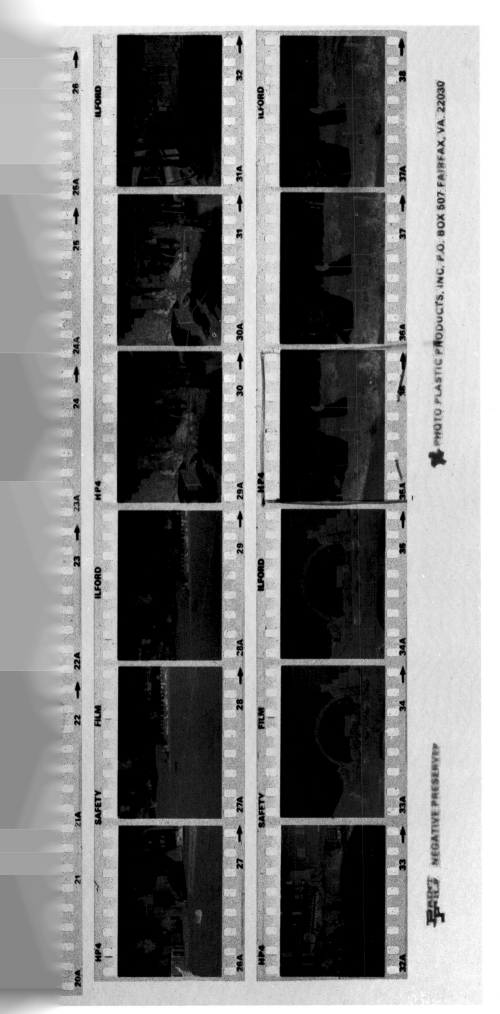

PHILIP PERKIS

I do not use contact sheets in my work. I prefer to work directly from negatives. It seems to me that I can visualize the print better by looking through a loupe at each negative.

Certain of my photographs, particularly of still subjects, tend to become fixed in my minds eye at the time they are made. The process then is simply to recognize the negative and make a fast print. The real editing of these pictures is to look at these prints over a long period of time, throwing away the ones that don't work out for any of several reasons.

The "creative" aspect of editing comes in finding a negative that is not remembered from the time of shooting (too fast, too complex, etc.). I seem to do this best by taking a stance as close to the shooting process as possible (just look!). I work with a small light box next to the enlarger: negatives spread out, and print for whatever reasons attract me (usually not logical or explainable, but just led by the eye to a "something"). This is the aspect of editing that seems to advance my vision. My average is low here, but without some element of chance I would soon lose interest.

The photograph reproduced is a perfect example of the "intuitive" choice in editing. I was attracted to the strong diagonal created by the metal bar and the fact that the placement of the figures fell into place when I saw the print. That was the real surprise.

PHILIP PERKIS

152

PETER SCHLESSINGER

First off . . . I don't use conventional-size contact sheets any more. After years of frustration and eyestrain I realized that my 8x10 sheets were tantalizing more than informing, and that I still had to print too many images just to find out if they were workable . . . so I got an old 8x10 enlarger that could projection-print a whole roll of 35mm film at once. Now, what I can see on the "contacts" is a good deal closer to what I'm likely to get in the print.

Second . . . what I choose from a contact sheet in a printing session has quite a bit to do with what I'm working on or toward at that moment. While I do believe in making images of all sorts at all times (responding as freely as possible to both what's "in front of me" and "what's on my mind" as well as being open to intuitive and symbolic combinations of the two) some images will clearly apply to a particular project or portfolio more than others. This doesn't invalidate the unprinted reminder . . . I may return to a sheet for other images that fit a different mold.

The contact sheet shown (partially) here is from a summer '79 shooting for the Long Island Project, a documentary study originated by Apeiron Workshops and funded by the National Endowment for the Arts and the Olympus Camera Corporation. Twelve photographers were working to get an "emotionally true image" of contemporary American life. I had assigned myself to do motor vehicles and associated lifestyles, as well as shooting more generally. The roll shown is the fourth of four done at the weekly biker's gathering at a drive-in restaurant in Oceanside, L.I. I was using an Olympus OM-2 without flash, utilizing its automatic exposure mode.

Frames 10A and 11A were taken near the rear of the lot; 12A was more towards the center. I like 10A for its sense of the attention and respect the machines are paid, and 12A for its rendering of the arc-light punk-surreality of the scene; 13A was in response to a take-my-picture look, and made me think of media imagery and the young . . . had they ever seen a Norton Motorcyle ad? 15A was a point-and-shoot (not looking through the viewfinder) in the midst of a lot of movement. 16A-17A-18A seem to record an archtypical "buzz off, kid" sexual triangulation; by the third frame the fellow on the left has asserted his proprietary rights to the motorcycle, at the very least. 19A and 20A were warm-ups for 21A, which is beauty-on-the-beast/innocence and asphalt . . . but it emulates what it tries to criticize (sex in motorcycle advertisements) too closely for clarity. 22A-23A-24A were for the bike owner who complained that I wasn't getting the whole machine in the pictures.

I decided to print two . . . 15A because it gave me the best feeling of "how it was" sensually; it has an implied audio component, and a kinetic simultanaeity that resonates with my memory of that night . . . and 18A, because it runs deeper, beyond sensory accuracy to something more mythic, something emotionally and descriptively true. I like it as social-sexual narrative: Mr. "Highway Collision" claims "The Blonde" and "The Kid" backs off . . . but "The Blonde" is aloof, looking coolly out of the frame at the viewer. I like how Mr. "H.C." and "The Blonde" are visually connected (his hand, her toe) . . . yet her other foot (bare) seems to reach out to "The Kid's" agitated hand. I like the light; I like the selective focus. I like the implied risk in being there as photographer and viewer. I may, of course, change my mind about the print later.

PETER SCHLESSINGER

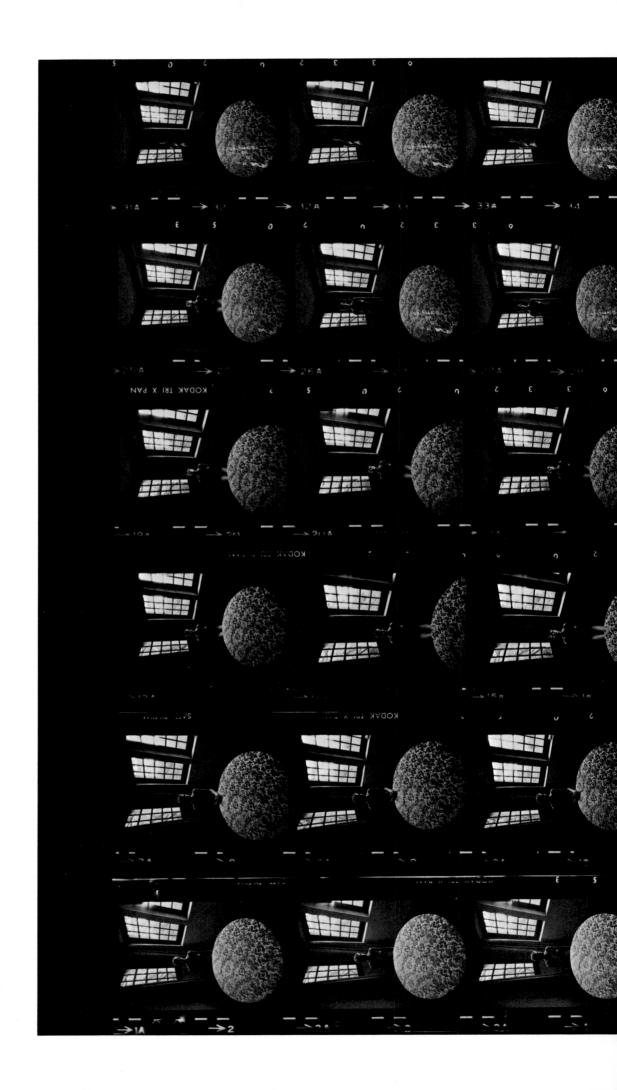

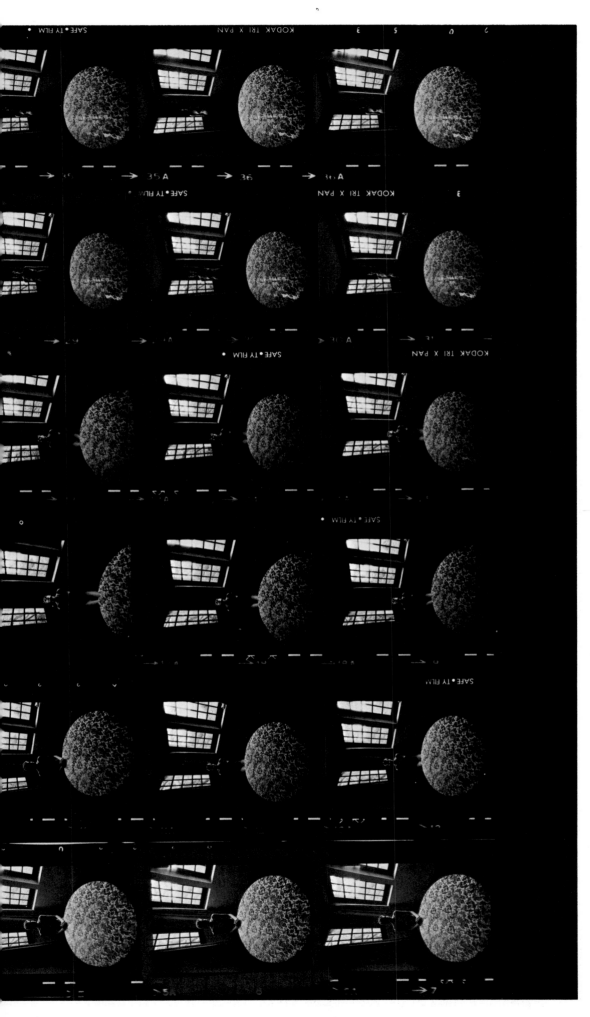

JEAN-LOUP SIEFF

My feelings about the contact sheets are strange, sometimes friendly, often conflicting.

I know that I took these photographs, and yet I discover with surprise, sometimes, some details I didn't remember, as if some new things were added that I didn't see when I took the photograph, and which I accept or reject when I choose the final photograph. Choice is a matter of the moment, of mood. Sometimes I make one choice one day and another a month later as if, as time passes, the photographs maintain their lives and continue to evolve.

In this contact sheet where I photographed a nude woman in an empty room, I chose five different points of view, but I don't always know which one I prefer, and my choice changes from day to day.

Choosing is for me hard work. I can often spend more than one hour going back and forth over the images, and what pleases me one day may displease me the next.

Other times the choice is evident, and appears immediately; everything is perfect, the composition, the expression, the light; but that rarely happens, alas. Finally, the time to choose is a moment that I fear, it is a lonely and hard struggle which exhausts me, often with regrets…."and is the other one better?"

Then to reassure myself, I repeat the old adage: "Don't trust your first impression, it is always the best!"

JEAN-LOUP SIEFF

EVE SONNEMAN

Body, Guatemala City, 1972

Festival day in Guatemala City was a high-spirited time. Something in the air was delirious. The night before there had been a coup in the city. Gunshots sounded like fireworks. Suddenly I came across a body, a solitary figure lying in the grass. Was it a dummy? A dead body? A sleeping figure? And why are those people staring? I didn't know so this definitely was the image I chose to print.

Sometimes I feel led like a magnet to a picture or a place presenting a picture. It occurs and feels just right. Senses at the time are the key for me. I must have remembered questions about that body when I returned home to New York. What puzzled and intrigued me in Guatemala City was what I decided to save as a visual image.

I printed two adjacent frames as I had done before and as I continued to do after "Body, Guatemala City." At the time (1972), combining adjacent frames was the clearest way I knew to show passage of time, location shifts, and my own involvement in image-making. I retained the bottom line of sprocket holes to show the connections between frames and the linear time passage. "Body, Guatemala City" and all other images in my book REAL TIME adhere to this theory.

Two years after this particular picture was made, I began to cut frames, combine black and white and color simultaneously, and alter radically the visual components of my pictures. I no longer used adjacent frames, but began altering time and free association between frames. My work became more open to interpretation as I invited the viewer to explore the real and imaginary world with me. It became imagined time, altered space. It became and still is becoming something adjacent to that delirious air!!!

EVE SONNEMAN

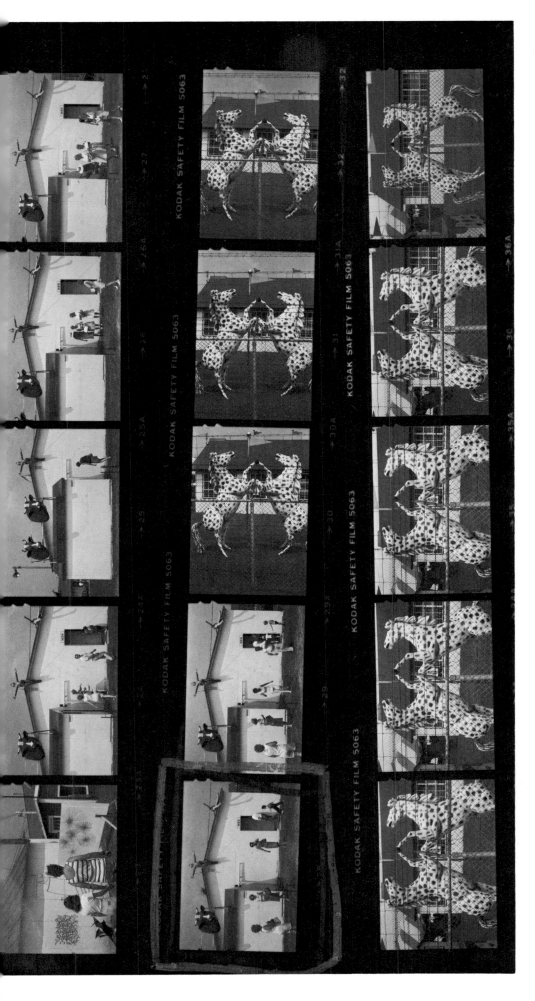

BURK UZZLE

Loose on a sunny afternoon, feeling good, spotted a place that had a twinkle.

The chuckles started well before the pictures; visual preconceptions, as always, started, slowed, faltered, and finally gave way to the strength of a good, honest picture overpowering the whole process.

The goofy architecture immediately presented itself as a theme and I hoped to add something to collaborate with the mood and place.

Started with obvious devices, placed with a plodding intelligence but little spark in all too logical places.

Regressed to corny humor and even a bout with tastelessness before giving way to a piss.

Sat down for a dose of sun and green grass and took a short nap.

Waking, still appreciative of a special place, and now under the influence of more spirit and less will, staring at a lovely picture that utterly insisted on being natural, spontaneous, and with a lovely essence of place and mood.

Stood up, pointed a normal lens on a ten year old Leica and managed, in spite of myself, to have that rich and joyful feeling when a good picture and I both know we have found each other.

The contact sheet at first disgusted me with all its stupidity. It's one of those sheets that reflects floundering within an idea. The one frame that works and is special was in a sequence that had found its way to be composed through trial and error, settled on, and then arrived at by watching and waiting for all the players to arrange themselves in a hospitable and interesting placement.

I saw geometry within the idea, within the essence of the place, within a sunny afternoon, and me almost without a picture.

Luckily and luck pursued discipline and patience, it all came together, only briefly, and we had fun together.

BURK UZZLE

7463
3/27/74

TX / HC-110

7 4 6 3 - 3        4        5

7 4 6 3 - 9.        1 0        1 1

7 4 6 3 - 1 5        1 6.        1 7

7 4 6 3 - 2 1.        2 2        2 3

DAVID VESTAL

Pickup & Dog, 7463-9

When we lived in northern New Mexico, I went out
to Spanish villages with Johnnie Martinez, a fine
photographer who was then with THE NEW MEXICAN, a
Santa Fe newspaper. Johnnie knows the territory and
speaks Spanish, things that helped.

Cordova is in a valley in the Sangre de Cristo
mountains. The people there were friendly but did
not want to be photographed, so we fell back on sun,
shade, dirt, tin roofs and adobe.

Two things that aren't pictures show in the contact
print. I use bulk film and load 30-shot rolls which fit
easily on 8x10; and I ink in information and frame
numbers on the film. India ink, unlike the photo
industry's frame numbers, always shows up clearly
on the proof.

Pictures: this sheet mostly shows the search, but
several frames got printed. Not frame No. 8. It shows
a place I liked, but which didn't work; a good stage
set, but no show. In frame No. 9, the dog came and
saved me.

DAVID VESTAL

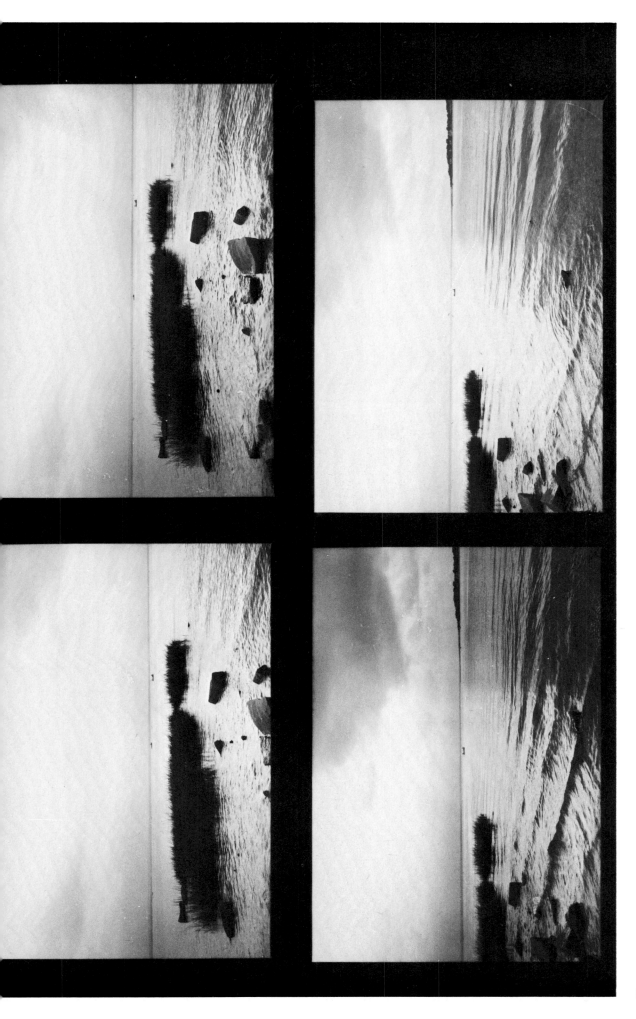

LARRY WHITE

The last time I made a contact sheet was seven years ago before I became a photojournalist. Even then I considered it a pain. So when I started having to meet deadlines it was a perfect excuse not to make contacts. I got pretty good at reading negatives.

With the recent increase in the cost of photo supplies I had to cut back on paper consumption somehow. Going back to making contacts seemed to be the answer. I wish I had always made them.

I use a custom-made 6 x 7 camera appropriately dubbed "the ugly rumor." It is a very lightweight, easy to handle camera, considering the negative size.

The nice thing is that the images on my contact sheets are big enough to be used as preliminary work prints. So I've started cutting out the "wallet size" pictures and I'm saving a great deal of paper.

Technically speaking, a contact sheet can tell me a great deal about how to print with a particular negative. I use a cold light enlarger which renders a print with the same tonal range as a contact sheet does. I know exactly how my negatives are going to print or what exposure and development adjustments might need to be made to get what I want. I only wish I had been proofing all along.

I was drawn to the four water images because of the light they emitted, exactly my experience of the day. The bottom two pictures worked formally and the final choice I made was because I could see the man in the front reaching out with his oar just breaking the water. That made the picture for me. It really put me out in that boat. Images of Huck Finn and Tom Sawyer floating down the Mississippi came back clear. I was there. It worked for me.

There are other images on the contact sheet that interest me. Primarily the upper left one of the yard. I printed it too, but it didn't sing like this one.

LARRY WHITE